"Richard Steckel is gifted, and <u>Filthy Rich</u> is a gift of wit and wisdom. Put aside the heavy business books and get <u>Filthy Rich</u>."

— Peter C. Brown, President
Peter C. Brown Associates
St. Paul, Minnesota

"In Richard Steckel's unabashedly unorthodox world, corporations care, non-profits profit, and people become the miracles that they are. In his own inimitable way, he is putting social action on the business agenda at the same time he helps the not-for-profit world survive. He's wonderful! Once he's in your life, things are never quite the same."

— Allie Bird
Director, Corporate Initiatives
National Crime Prevention Council
Washington, D.C.

"It's great to work with someone who makes cents."

— Louise Donovan
Public Relations/
Financial Development Director
Vancouver YWCA
Vancouver, BC, Canada

"Richard Steckel's legendary creativity, wit, and wisdom are available in abundance in this book. Steckel, Simons and Lengsfelder write from the experience of successful entrepreneurs, with the insight of true visionaries in this important field. No entrepreneur, whether in the for-profit or not-for-profit sector, should miss this book. It is helpful, practical, funny, positive and altogether irresistible. It is the most engaging work of art to appear since Mona Lisa's smile."

— Thomas A. Barron
President and Chief Operating Officer
The Prospect Group
New York, New York

"Without a doubt, Richard Steckel is the best in the field. I have been proud to bring Richard out to Washington, Oregon and Alaska. As a result, hundreds of nonprofit organizations have learned to become financially more self-reliant."

— Kumi Kilburn
Former Vice President
Social Policy
Rainier National Bank
Seattle, Washington

"Steckel's ideas make money to fund good causes."

— Michael Ainslie
President and
Chief Executive Officer
Sotheby's Holding Company
New York, New York

"Richard Steckel is at his irreverent, communicative best. Through humor, spice and tales of woe, he nevertheless walks nonprofits through the reality of operating a business venture in the charitable sector . . . deserves attention."

—Thomas Jones, President
Enterprise Fund, Inc.
Washington, D.C.

FILTHY RICH AND OTHER NONPROFIT FANTASIES

Changing the way nonprofits do business in the 90's

by
Dr. Richard Steckel
with Robin Simons and Peter Lengsfelder

Ten Speed Press

TEN SPEED PRESS
P.O. Box 7123
Berkeley, California 94707

Book and Cover Design by Design and Image Communications, Inc., Denver, Colorado
Typesetting by Campro, Denver, Colorado

MONOPOLY game equipment and artwork used with permission from Parker Brothers © 1935, 1985.

Lyrics to "MY SHOES" © 1986 by Richard Greene, Gunnar Madsen, and Mark Pritchard, Best of Breed Music-ASCAP. Reprinted by permission.

"THE WAY YOU DO THE THINGS YOU DO" by William Robinson & Robert Rogers. © 1964 by Jobete Music Co., Inc. Reprinted with permission.

Library of Congress Cataloging-in-Publication Data

Steckel, Richard.
    Filthy rich and other non-profit fantasies/Richard Steckel, Peter Lengsfelder & Robin Simons.
    p. cm.
    ISBN 0-89815-267-4 (pbk.)
    1. Corporations, Nonprofit—Management.   2. Corporations, Nonprofit—Finance.
I. Lengsfelder, Peter. II. Simons, Robin. III. Title.
HD62.6.S74 1988
658.1'148—dc19   88-26045
                  CIP

Printed in the United States of America

4   5   6   7   8   9   10   —   97   96   95   94

CONTENTS

PART IV   VENTURES: MAKING THE FANTASY REAL

PART V   VEHICLES: DRIVING THE FANTASY HOME

FOREWORD

Fantasy is the free play of imagination. It means letting go of old ideas and patterns, and searching unlikely places for useful new ones. That's why we've tickled this book with Gary Cooper, The New Jersey Division of Gaming Enforcement, the Archbishop of Canterbury, even Yogi Berra. Valuable insights come out of left field, if you're open to them.

Still, we know letting go isn't easy, and trying new things is just as tough. (Buying our first phone answering machine was a monumental decision. Now it's an indispensable member of the family!) But nonprofits have important work to do and no time to waste fighting the inexorable forces of change. Instead you need to grab every available tool and trend; anything that enables you to get on with your work and deliver your mission. Your work should flow.

This book will show you how the most successful nonprofits find the flow of enterprise by trusting their fantasies and borrowing tools from the private sector. It will show you how successful nonprofits use enterprise to get their messages heard, their missions met. And it will help you to do the same.

In the back of our book, you will find an Enterprise Worksheet. It will help you plot the strategy for making your fantasy real. We'll evaluate it for free if you send it in. Between now and the time you reach that worksheet, you have nothing to do but read, enjoy and set free your imagination.

Nonprofit Enterprise: Who Says You Can't Fantasize?

CHAPTER 1:

Changing The Way You Do Business

"The trouble with being poor
is that it takes up all your time."
—Willem de Kooning,
artist

This book is about changing your nonprofit organization from a poor, grant-dependent, sand-kicked-in-your-face operation into one that is muscular and self-reliant. It is about paying your own way with earned income ventures, and about using those ventures to improve the delivery of your mission.

This book is also about changing the skinny way you think. For too long, nonprofits have been bound by assumptions that limit their effectiveness. No more. A new class of nonprofits has developed, with muscular attitudes and behaviors borrowed from the private sector. The private sector provides some excellent role models; just because they're brawny doesn't mean they're bad guys. So let's throw out your tacit tongue *tssks* right now.

We'll show you how to develop an entrepreneurial nonprofit, one that is goal and customer oriented. You will learn how to shape a strong, practical vision. You will see for yourself that your nonprofit can be innovative, risk-taking and solvent; ventures will earn you predictable and unrestricted operating income. Above all, this book will help you sell your mission—to broader audiences than you've ever dreamed.

LICENSE TO DREAM

Look what other people have dreamed up over the past few years: Power ties. Hulk Hogan. Passive exercise. Chocolate encounter groups. Madonna! We all got here, to this improbable place of other people's fantasies, through marketing. Still, so many important issues go unresolved while people are out walking their pet Gucci's. Nonprofits, especially, seem to be having a hard time being heard.

Why?

Because your fantasy has been weighted down by the seriousness of your mission; your fantasy has taken a bum rap. Some people talk about fantasy as if it were an outdated concept, maybe even a dangerous one. As if it distracts you from reality. Quit daydreaming, they say. Come down to Earth. Get on with business.

In fact, fantasy has lots to do with business—especially yours. Imagining is the business of nonprofits. It is the imagination that sees a more equitable, more productive world. It is the first step toward creating change. How else are we going to feed the hungry? Or cure the sick? Shelter the homeless? Retrain troubled youth? Assist the disabled? Prevent crime? Nonprofits know all about fantasy. That's where their goals begin.

THE END AT THE BEGINNING

Unfortunately, that's also where fantasy ends for most nonprofits: at the beginning. Missions are sparked and sculpted from fantasy, but when it comes to the politic and business of carrying out those missions, nonprofits have traditionally floundered; they can't produce results the way the private sector does; they become traditionalists; they become the Invisible Sector. Irritating, isn't it?

There are a bunch of traditional assumptions you've been lugging around, assumptions about how nonprofits operate. To show you how universal these assumptions are, we've made a list, and we'll bet you can separate the 7 nonprofit grindstones from the others.

		"X" HERE IF THIS
	ASSUMPTIONS	SOUNDS NONPROFIT
1.	Money will always be a problem	( )
2.	We will always be grant dependent	( )
3.	We will always need some Smokey Robinson and the Miracles	( )
4.	We will always be tied to funders' priorities and schedules	( )
5.	We should take the pitch on 3 and 0	( )
6.	We can't go back to Constantinople	( )
7.	There will be long lag times between getting a grant and getting the money	( )
8.	Our staff will always be overworked and underpaid	( )
9.	We're dependent on volunteers who aren't always effective	( )
10.	Hawaii is effective	( )
11.	We can't afford to go to Hawaii very often	( )
12.	We can't afford to do projects the way we would like	( )

Now let's tally up your score.

If you chose Assumptions #3, 5, 6, 10 and 11, then you've got a distorted sense of grindstones. It's the other assumptions that are limiting your power.

Look at the assumptions again. Highlight them with a yellow marker. You may want to change the world, but assumptions like these—thinking like this—is tying your hands. Thinking like this limits your ability to earn money, to reach new audiences, to adapt to change—to deliver your mission. Believing those assumptions condemns you to live them. It means you'll always be left on the beach or standing in line for the leftovers.

NEW NONPROFIT ASSUMPTIONS

Cheer up. Many nonprofits have learned not to operate under those traditional assumptions. They are becoming productive. In fact, in the last two decades, the Labor Department reports that the nonprofit sector has grown faster than either private business or the government. Enterprising nonprofits have followed their fantasies, and their fantasies have released them from assumptions; have freed them to scout new ways of accomplishing their objectives. You can too; you can decide where you want to go and at what pace.

Take a closer look at your organization and you're likely to find fantasies already floating around, even if you haven't checked on them for a while. Don't some of your fantasies look like this?:

THE FILTHY RICH FANTASY

1. We'll have lots of unrestricted cash.

2. The money will be spaced evenly throughout the year.

3. We'll use the revenues for projects of our own choosing.

4. Revenues will cover our general operating costs.

OTHER NONPROFIT FANTASIES

1. We will reach huge audiences with our mission and message.

2. We will pay our staff competitive salaries.

3. Our staff won't be chronically overworked.

4. We will be the best organization in our field.

5. We will effect change.

It's time to talk about those fantasies in the light of day, not stash them away as ties to a world that probably was never as good as it is remembered. Realize your fantasies by changing the way you do business, by dropping the onerous nonprofit assumptions and embracing some productive assumptions from the private sector. As Yogi Berra once said, "You can observe a lot just by watching."

NEW NONPROFIT ASSUMPTIONS

1. **Nonprofits can operate like businesses.** By adopting for-profit attitudes and behaviors, nonprofits can strengthen the way they operate, the way they serve their customers, the way they meet their goals, the way they deliver their missions.

2. **Nonprofits can have a clear vision of the future and a clear path for getting there.** By being proactive rather than reactive, nonprofits can anticipate changes in funding and market needs, they can monitor trends and plan accordingly.

We're going to assist you in making these new assumptions second nature. In doing so, your nonprofit fantasies will become reality. Your nonprofit can be customer-centered, always looking for the next need, with new and better ways to fill that need. Your staff won't have to be underpaid and overworked; by offering incentives and rewards, nonprofits can keep staff motivated and pay salaries commensurate with the private sector. Your audiences are not all poor; by broadening your view of whom you serve, your nonprofit can develop new, paying audiences for its programs. You don't have to wait and compete for funders' handouts. By developing programs that meet businesses' needs you can *earn* money from corporations, put them to work for you, and isn't it about time for that!

Stay loose and read on.

CHAPTER 2:

Why Now? Why Me?

"The fastest way to succeed is to look as if
you're playing by other people's rules,
while quietly playing by your own."
—Michael Korda,
author

Your fantasy is in jeopardy. Never before has the question of your motivation been so relevant. Are you here to effect change or talk about it? For nonprofits serious about their missions, there is precious little time for the gloriously-worded mission statements of the 1960's. Not unless you can back it up with good old-fashioned enterprise. Enterprise must be part of the equation because the only thing that still resembles 1960 is Dick Clark.

NOUVELLE FUNDRAISING

Fundraising was once meat and potatoes for most nonprofits. It was never easy scrapping together a full plate, but those times seem halcyon compared with today's nouvelle fare: eentsy portions of "greens," served with a sprig of good wishes for better luck elsewhere. The belt-tightening of the Reagan Administration seasoned an international trend that made it even more difficult to raise money. Yet it's the truly hungry and enterprising nonprofits that make use of these trends. They don't fight them. They relish them.

Here is some food for thought: the following are the forces growling at your stomach, that you feel at work...

8 WAYS TO REDUCE A NONPROFIT

GOVERNMENT RETRENCHMENT: With reductions in domestic spending, government is cutting back on contracts to human service agencies. To be exact, $27 billion since 1980! These contracts have been the lifeblood of many nonprofits. The decline in government funding forces these agencies to consider cutbacks of their own and to compete with the ever-growing number of nonprofits for private funding sources.

PRIVATIZATION: At the same time that government is stepping out of public service, the private sector is stepping in. Postal service, correctional facilities, health care, elder care, child care, transportation of the elderly and handicapped, braille translation, and other traditional nonprofit areas are being invaded by private enterprise. As government contracts decline, more agencies are forced to turn to private sources for operating funds.

MERGERS and ACQUISITIONS: In 1987 9,000 corporations were bought out or merged, pulling $4 million dollars from the grant pool. While there is a simultaneous burgeoning of small business, the fledgling companies are not financially stable enough to replace the grant monies lost in the mergers. The result is a slowdown in the growth of the grant pool at exactly the same time that nonprofit demands are increasing. The Fortune 500 may soon be the Fortune 50, and what's more, corporate contributions are flat for the first time in 20 years!

ACCOUNTABILITY: As competition among nonprofits increases, funders are forced to make difficult choices between them. To choose wisely, many funding sources now scrutinize nonprofits more closely. They want to avoid duplication of efforts, so they give money to organizations that have the greatest impact. Unfortunately, giving to the most deserving has frequently meant giving to the most stable. As a result, young and experimental agencies without strong track records are slighted in the grant-making process. To relieve the pressure on their limited funds, some granting agencies have actually begun urging closure of nonprofits with chronic deficits or shaky management. Other grantors lobby for mergers of groups providing similar services. Of course, funders can't force an organization to close, but they can make operation difficult by curtailing the cash.

THE SHIFT TO STRATEGIC PHILANTHROPY: Corporate giving is increasingly becoming a marketing strategy in which companies fund projects that promise the greatest publicity or financial return. Self-interest and *quid pro quo* have become bywords. This makes it harder for nonprofits to raise operating cash and to find support for projects that lack a strong publicity angle.

COMPASSION FATIGUE: In 1987 Elizabeth Taylor complained that it was getting harder to raise money for AIDS research and services. AIDS had ceased to be the "fashionable charity," despite the disease's still-rising fatalities. It had followed Farm Aid, Band Aid, Live Aid, children, handicaps and model cities into — and out of — the funding limelight. Individuals, as well as governments and foundations, expect simple solutions to complex problems. It's a "flavor-of-the-year" mentality. We gave to that last year, let's try a different one this year — though the problem continues to exist.

COMPETITION OF SORROWS: As competition for limited funds gets tougher, nonprofits find themselves in a debilitating competition of sorrows. In a world where dollars go to the organization with the worthiest cause, organizations vie to be the most desperate in need; the saddest in story; the one with the desolate eyes on the cover of their fundraising brochure. How many organizations can compete with a children's hospital? It's a competition most nonprofits are bound to lose.

DIGESTING THE HAND THAT FEEDS: As operating costs increase faster than grant dollars, nonprofits are forced to turn repeatedly to their members — we sometimes refer to this as incest fundraising — and donors for money. The organization adds a mid-year fundraising appeal; they increase the price of membership; they up the cost of admission. Sure, the strategy works — for a while. Soon they reach a point of diminishing returns: members and donors grow weary, alienation sets in. The nonprofit loses its most valuable constituents. Clearly, new sources of money need to be found.

These trends compound the existing problems of relying on fundraised dollars: (1) the money is almost always restricted in its use; (2) it is slow in coming with long lag times between applying for a grant, getting approval and getting the funds; (3) organizations must tie their requests to funders' priorities, often foregoing their real needs and interests; and (4) funding is tied to grantmaking cycles, resulting in uneven, uncontrollable cash flow.

BREAD AND BUTTER BACKERS

To mitigate grant problems, some nonprofits have begun looking to their bread and butter supporters — their constituents. Problem is, many find that cupboard bare, too, because they're looking in the wrong place: the past.

In the past, nonprofit constituents were children of the Depression. To them, "Smoke Gets In Your Eyes" was beautiful music and Tyrone Power was The Star. To them, money was the valued commodity. They were wooed by the promise of a "bargain" or a "good deal." Nonprofits met this need with memberships, subscriptions and multiple services at discount prices. They came to depend on those tools as perennial sources of income.

Today's major consumers and nonprofit constituents are careful not to overdue the bread and butter. To them, (cigarette) "Smoke Gets In Your Eyes" is a battle cry and BMW horsepower makes The Star. They're Babyboomers, and Babyboomers are different. With well-paying jobs and double incomes, many of the 76 million Boomers have considerable disposable income. What they lack is time. Struggling to balance careers, family and recreation, they value freedom, convenience and flexibility rather than monetary savings. They will go to the theater for a single performance, but they won't commit to a year's subscription. They will go to a museum when the show is a blockbuster, but they won't buy a membership. Their values and spending patterns are different from past generations. Offers of dollar value that place demands on their time, fall on Walkman-muffled ears.

As a result, nonprofits are finding that not only have their traditional sources of grant funding dried up, so have their in-house sources. For the first time we're seeing scores of nonprofits filing for reorganization and protection from creditors under Chapter 11. Some are even filing for bankruptcy.

BEND AN EAR AND OTHER PARTS

The solution is to watch and listen. Then be flexible, use your imagination. Recognize that grant money probably can't be counted on to provide the majority of your support anymore. Creative nonprofits are pliable nonprofits. They are beginning to actively recruit new audiences and acknowledge their audiences' changing needs. That means not only changing what they offer but also the way they offer it.

Several theaters, for instance, are now providing child care with their performances so young parents can bring their children. Many offer dinner/theater packages, so Boomers wanting a night on the town can get it conveniently pre-arranged. Some offer a new subscription model, in which patrons advance-purchase a block of tickets — but the nights the tickets are usable are not predetermined. This meets the theaters' need for guaranteed cash and the audience's need for flexibility.

Recognizing that standard exhibition techniques intimidate many people, museums have begun using more theatrical displays and more live programming. Such strategies help the museums convey their message more effectively to wider audiences.

Recognizing that young parents are vitally interested in their children's education, museums have begun offering more hands-on activities and more children's programs. These additions attract new visitors and build audiences for the future.

Recognizing Babyboomers' need for an alternative to the bar scene, ballets and orchestras are hosting cash bars before performances. These defacto singles events bring new audiences to the theaters *and* boost concessions revenue.

The key, of course, is not to rely on business as usual. Avoid the headon disasters that are starving so many nonprofits. Loosen your grip on assumptions and welcome trends as creative advantages. Examine your audiences' needs. Are there matchups that you can offer?

There are salad days on the horizon. The nonprofits above have strengthened both the delivery of their missions and their bottom lines. Their flexible, proactive, market-oriented approach bodes well for their organizations' futures. They have become entrepreneurial nonprofits.

CHAPTER 3:

Words Will Never Hurt Me: Call It Entrepreneurial

"When people don't want to come,
nothing will stop them."
—Sol Hurok
impresario

Who wants to use words like entrepreneurial when there are easier ones to work with? Try responsive. Try customer centered. Try flexible. These are the starting points and should be the core of how most nonprofits think.

What this means is that you believe your mission must be heard through the Roar and Clutter of headlines, magazine ads, junk mail, TV commercials, phone call solicitations, billboards and everything else that bombards us daily. How will you navigate that traffic? How will you get through to people with your message?

Entrepreneurial nonprofits choose the mainstream roads. Traditional nonprofits take the side roads. Who's delivering the message? Let's take a look at the two approaches.

MARKET-DRIVEN DRIVERS

Entrepreneurial nonprofits know they must be responsive — and responsible — to their markets. They enjoy serving people. That's where they get their power. They ask their audiences, "What do you want, how are we doing?" If they get off course, they ask their audiences for direction. They are "market driven." They stay flexible, sensing change early, then watching and using it to their advantage.

BUMPER CAR MENTALITY

Traditional nonprofits, on the other hand, are "program driven." They've put their programs in the driver's seat, audience in the back, and they drive the side roads diligently. Unfortunately, the route doesn't change regardless of who the audience is or where it wants to go. New audiences develop but, steered by their programs, the nonprofits don't see them and can't meet their needs. These nonprofits are captive to the side roads as bumper cars are to an arena.

Traditional nonprofits could "afford" this Bumper Car Mentality because in the oval arena overhead power was supplied by funders. It didn't matter if the audience tired;

invariably there was The Grant. Audiences weren't always adequately served, or served efficiently. Nobody seemed to notice.

DRIVING THE DOLLAR

However, funding tightened; now nonprofits need more money at the door. They're faced with fear: will the Dollar drive them? Will it detour their mission? Entrepreneurial nonprofits know that market responsiveness strengthens their purpose; it enables them to serve multiple audiences and serve them better! Their market-driven programs can generate sufficient income to support programs that won't pay for themselves.

Entrepreneurial nonprofits like money rather than fear it. They hire people from the public or private sector who are comfortable with money and who have strong financial skills. "We want people who understand that this organization should be run like a business," says the national vice president of personnel for the American Cancer Society.

Solid financial people know they have to earn their keep. The good ones uphold their concern for quality and service in the face of economic pressure. They turn occasional tensions between program and marketing staffs into productive energy. They use money to enhance the quality and delivery of their programs. They drive The Dollar, not the other way around.

VIRGINITY, POLLUTION & THE FILTHY RICH

Meanwhile, traditional nonprofits are distrustful of money. Many disagree with the "bottom line" thinking of the for-profit world. They fear that if concerned with money, they will lose their social goals. They fear money will pollute their mission. They fear they will lose their nonprofit virginity.

Symptomatic of that fear is their avoidance of for-profit terms. The word "profit," for instance, never appears on a nonprofit's budget. Oh no. Instead you see words like "excess over expenses." (Saving money is one area where nothing succeeds like excess.) Local organizations that report to national offices never call themselves "franchises" even though operationally many are. Managers in nonprofits are called "directors" and "assistant directors" rather than "presidents" and "vice presidents."

Even our title, *Filthy Rich*, probably illicits uncomfortable reaction from many traditional nonprofits, as if do-good organizations shouldn't have a lot of cash. Or is it because they think it suggests they've earned the money dishonorably? Lighten up! The useful and honorable in our society deserve rewards, too.

Being afraid of words or money doesn't make sense when you have a difficult mission ahead. You have enough to think about. *If* you become rich, be useful with your riches. Fact is, the filthy part of our fantasy has nothing to do with money. Rather it means getting into the trenches a little, getting dirty a little, maybe even getting roughed up a little because you're willing to take a chance and try new approaches.

Discomfort with money even extends to fundraising where some nonprofits differentiate between "clean" and "dirty" money, refusing to accept money from businesses they don't believe in. Unfortunately, some of the least desirable businesses are the ones that are the most philanthropic. (Imagine the art world without Philip Morris.)

We're certainly not suggesting that you trample your ethical standards in pursuit of money. We *are* suggesting that few financial choices are black and white. As corporations move in and out of industries and countries, it gets harder to remember who's clean and who's not.

Once you believe your mission must be heard through the Roar and the Clutter, you must be aggressive in pursuit of it. Entrepreneurial nonprofits realize that money is money. It's neither clean nor dirty; it's merely a tool to be used. Entrepreneurial nonprofits control it, not the other way around.

Entrepreneurial nonprofits like money rather than fear it.

Risky Business

More than anything Anita McKeowan wants to be a cop. According to the Orange County Register, she's willing to accept the risks that come with it. Her first probationary year on the force, the Santa Monica (CA) police officer encountered problems in the police academy with a dislocated shoulder and a rattlesnake bite. She also hurt her back and broke her finger while on patrol when she wrestled with a drunken driver who tried to run away.

Six weeks later, McKeowan was stabbed repeatedly in the chest when questioning a man about making too much neighborhood noise. A bulletproof vest saved her life, but her hand was badly cut. A second man put a gun to her head and pulled the trigger, but the weapon only clicked. Instead she was clubbed over the head and sent to the hospital.

When McKeowan returned to work, a drunken driver ran through red flares and smashed into her. After a six-week hiatus and 23 days on the job, McKeowan was pulling over a car for a broken tail-light when its passenger fired several shots into her patrol car. A wild chase ensued.

In the crash that ended the chase, McKeowan suffered a broken ankle and sternum, a bruised heart and blurred vision.

"I just hope next year is not like this year," said the determined McKeowan.

If you want to be where the action is, you've got to take risks. Only you can establish the level of the stakes, but one fact is clear:

Entrepreneurial nonprofits are comfortable with risk. In considering a new program or expense, they know that certainty is impossible. After a reasonable amount of research and planning, they trust their intuition and act. This enables them to capitalize on market opportunities. "Whenever you see a successful business," it's been said, "someone once made a courageous decision."

TYRANNY OF CERTAINTY

Traditional nonprofits, on the other hand, tend to fear risk. They want certainty before making big decisions. They have a preoccupation with checking off lists. Since life doesn't provide guarantees, this Tyranny of Certainty further retards the decision making process and encourages inaction.

Nonprofits fear risk for two reasons. One is its lack of affordability: they can't afford to lose operating cash by trying new, unguaranteed ventures. Fortunately that's not always necessary. Many entrepreneurial nonprofits have realized that by using the cash of their corporate partners, they need not risk their own. The second reason is a more generalized fear of failure. Trying something new has its dangers, and no one likes to fail. Entrepreneurial nonprofits have realized that failure is just one step in the learning process, one step toward success. They know the only real failure is failure to act at all.

 Entrepreneurial nonprofits are comfortable with risk.

> A manager at IBM was given $10 million to develop a new program. After a year the venture failed. Resolutely, the manager brought his letter of resignation to his boss who replied, "Resign? We won't let you resign. We just spent $10 million educating you!"

STREAMLINED STRATEGIES

Entrepreneurial nonprofits are action-oriented. They know where they are going and are impatient to get there. In order to make quick decisions, they've streamlined their decision-making process so that only people vital to the decision are involved. They are able to compress the lag time between decision and implementation. They've brought together a team of like-minded players who can quickly conceptualize and develop fantasies into practical programs, products or services. This also allows them to be opportunistic, to watch for and seize opportunities that appear.

TYRANNY OF DEMOCRACY

Traditional nonprofits, however, tend to be preoccupied with planning. They make decisions slowly, subjecting each decision to endless, and often unnecessary, opinions in a paralyzing Tyranny of Democracy. Passionate ideas are sucked dry in the process. (See Chapter 31.)

FANTASY VS. FANTASIA

Entrepreneurial nonprofits have leaders rather than managers. Leaders have a vision. Through their own passion and optimism, they inspire people to work toward implementing it. Leaders give direction rather than directions. They trust their staffs to meet their high expectations, and continually demonstrate that trust. They encourage decision-making by staff, by giving them responsibility and authority to act. They empower their staffs by removing obstacles. They manage by asking questions. They listen to the answers.

Leaders see themselves as teachers. They expect their staffs to grow, and challenge them to do so. They praise naturally and sincerely, and make everyone feel like winners. Leaders are role models for their staffs, leading by example. They are not afraid to say: "I don't know," "I need help," or "I was wrong."[1]

Leaders love a challenge — even challenges to themselves. They consider conflict healthy and encourage discussion. But they deal quickly with tensions, not allowing them to fester.

Leaders see both the grand design and the specifics of implementing it. Because they are competitive with themselves, they sometimes set goals that are unrealistic.

Leaders value change rather than fear it, because change encourages creativity and improvement.

Traditional nonprofits tend to follow a different approach. Just as in Walt Disney's *Fantasia*, wherein Mickey Mouse was the Sorcerer's Apprentice, staff are often guided by fixed tasks without knowing the eventual goal. Mickey conjured up one of the sorcerer's magic spells and set the brooms to carrying buckets of water from the well into the castle. They kept coming mindlessly with buckets and buckets and buckets of water. Mickey almost drowned because of it. Mickey had no vision, and offered none to his staff, so the goal was lost.

"Nice guys finish last."
—Leo "The Lip" Durocher,
baseball manager

NO MORE MR. NICE GUY

Entrepreneurial nonprofits expect and demand the best. Being nice isn't good enough. These are the folks with inherent designer genes. They define themselves as the best in their fields and consistently hire the best staff and contractors to help them realize that vision.

Traditional nonprofits, unfortunately, have a second class mentality. Some say they have an excess number of humility genes. In the name of affordability, they tolerate being less successful than the private sector. They hire cheaper designers for their newsletters, cheaper architects for their buildings, cheaper staffs for their programs. The subtle message is that they don't deserve or expect the best, and that message is heard loud and clear by their staffs, their publics and their funders.

One of the cruelest by-products of this attitude is the willingness to retain non-performing staff. Thinking it's kinder, managers retain people well after it's time for them to leave. The person usually knows what's coming, as does everyone around him. To make them wait and wonder is unfair, irritating, and poisonous to the organization.

The same is true for volunteers. Nonprofits have a tendency to let their goodwill toward volunteers impede the delivery of their missions. They let volunteers slow the organization and lower its standards. Volunteers begin to think that because they're free they can't be fired. A bad volunteer does more harm than good. Don't accept mediocrity, unless you believe you deserve it.

ALTERATIONS WHILE YOU WAIT

Entrepreneurial nonprofits anticipate change. They realize the world is always changing; to meet their goals they must change with it. So they look ahead, they watch for trends, they plan for change, they are prepared. Again, this allows organizations to be opportunistic, to watch for and seize opportunity when it presents itself. Entrepreneurial nonprofits appreciate change because they see it as an opportunity for growth and learning.

Traditional nonprofits tend to fear change. Once they establish their mission, they follow it loyally, without reevaluating it to see if needs have changed. Rather than anticipating change, they wait for it to hit them. Then market changes, funding changes, political changes, catch them unaware. With a thud.

Entrepreneurial nonprofits anticipate change.

SEEING IS BELIEVING

Entrepreneurial nonprofits have a clear vision of the future and of how they will get there. The vision is concrete, quantifiable and operational; it describes what they'll do and how they'll do it; it defines the style of the organization. The vision is actively communicated, internally and externally. It motivates staff, galvanizes the public and attracts investors because it paints achievable pictures of success. The vision grows and changes because it is the organization's living definition. It is universally understood, constantly talked about, and frequently challenged.

Traditional nonprofits, on the other hand, have mission statements. These spell out their broadest goals in terms that are unmeasurable and frequently unachievable. ("We strive for an end to discrimination.") Rather than becoming motivated, the staff cowers from the unmanageable task ahead, often unable to take a first step, for the mission statement provides no direction. Nor is the public inspired by such statements: talk is cheap. As a result, mission statements sit in drawers, unchanged and rarely consulted from year to year. Mission statements are important – but boring. Every organization should have one. But entrepreneurial nonprofits need visions too.

ROAD TO GLORY

All these non-traditional characteristics position nonprofits to take advantage of market opportunities. They enable the enterprising organization to match its skills and expertise with the needs of its audiences; to deliver its programs in ways that are profitable.

These qualities also open a nonprofit to a new, lucrative, avenue for reaching people. That avenue is corporations.

You may be used to seeing corporations exclusively as funders, but entrepreneurial nonprofits see and use corporations as something else: as buyers. Corporations can purchase products and services, then distribute them to their own large networks of customers and employees. Suddenly corporations are not just sources of contributions, not even just sources of earned income. They are powerful business partners who, in mutually beneficial ventures, apply their own marketing strength, finances and savvy to spreading a nonprofit's mission.

Remember, entrepreneurial nonprofits . . .

Like money rather than fear it.

Are comfortable with risk.

Are action-oriented.

Have leaders rather than managers.

Expect and demand the best.

Anticipate change.

Have a clear vision of the future and how they will get there.

CHAPTER 4:

Using Corporations To Advance Your Goals

PICK-THE-PARTNER GAME

Directions for the game: Match the nonprofit and its venture partner.

Nonprofit

1. **"Up With People" Tour**
   Performed in 37 cities as a birthday present for company employees and families.

Betty Friedan/author

James D. Robinson/CEO; American Express Corp.

2. **National Trust for Historic Preservation**
   Receives licensing fees for duplication of historic wallpaper and fabric patterns found in its classic homes.

PeeWee Herman

3. **Free To Be You & Me Foundation**
   Packaged and sold the reknowned "Free To Be You & Me" record, book, tape, TV show and all subsequent spinoffs for licensing royalties.

4. **New York Metropolitan Opera**
   For a fee of $250,000, allowed a new product to be introduced to its upscale audience at an opening night gala.

Bob Solomon/Applause

5. **Children's Television Workshop**
   Licensed the Sesame Street characters products that now generate over $30 million annually for CTW.

6. **Museum of Modern Art (New York City)**
   Sold the air rights above its building for $17,000,000.

Nancy Reagan

7. **Cape Hatteras Lighthouse**
   Allowed this partner to use revitalization of the lighthouse in its marketing campaign in exchange for a contribution.

Marlo Thomas/A&M

Philip P. Puschel, CEO and President, F. Schumacher & Co.

Answers: 1 — Honeywell Corporation 2 — F.Schumacher & Co. 3 — Marlo Thomas/A&M Record Co. 4 — Chanel Perfumes 5 — Bob Solomon/Applause 6 — Charles Shaw/Developer 7 — American Express Co.

Is it strange to think of corporations as your customers? As buyers of nonprofit products and services? Especially when donation dollars are shrinking? It shouldn't be. Two recent trends in the corporate sector make this seemingly unusual relationship more and more common. Corporate spending is up in these areas:

A) Employee Relations

B) Marketing

In both areas, corporations are finding nonprofits profitable beneficiaries of their spending.

EMPLOYEE RELATIONS

Corporations are increasingly sensitive to losses in productivity, especially those caused by employee problems and concerns. Drug and alcohol abuse, child care, care for aging parents and crime, all distract employees from their jobs. To stem these losses, businesses are bringing rehabilitation, counseling and support services into the worksite. This is part of a slowly growing trend to broaden employee benefits, to attract and retain a quality work force, and to demonstrate corporate concern for its employees beyond the work day. Nonprofits that can creatively offer services to employees can take advantage of this trend.

For example, Eldercare, a nonprofit in Somerville (MA), contracts with corporations to assist employees who have an aging parent at home. Among its services are seminars, telephone counseling, and community resource referrals.

MARKETING

The second area in which nonprofits are partnering with corporations is marketing. Nonprofits, by virtue of their social-serving missions, are endowed by the public with a host of positive attributes. They are seen as unselfish, caring, committed, honest, and a variety of other qualities that vary with the organization's goals. Museums are seen as cultured, high-brow and distinguished; environmentalists as gutsy, outdoorsy and having the courage of their convictions. Additionally, each individual nonprofit has its own list of positive qualities that defines its personality.

Corporations are not so lucky. Their goal is to make money, so they are often seen as self-serving and uncaring — qualities not terribly endearing to customers. Thus, corporations appreciate their associations with nonprofits. In a wide variety of marketing partnerships, corporations in effect "rent" the positive qualities of the nonprofit to improve their image with the buying public. Nonprofits make corporations look good to consumers.

For example, in 1984, American Express approached the Statue of Liberty with an idea for a donation campaign. The statue just stood there, but her restoration committee responded. During a three-month period, American Express agreed to give $1 of each purchase made with an American Express card, and $5 from each new card application, to the Statue's restoration fund. American Express bargained that by tying their donation to card use, they would make money for the Statue and for themselves as well. They were right.

During the three months of the campaign they raised $1.7 million for the Statue, and American Express card use rose 28%. New card applications rose 17%. The success of the campaign spawned hundreds of similar for-profit/nonprofit partnerships. Corporate marketing departments were realizing the power of association – association with a nonprofit cause. Who would have dreamt? Well, someone did.

All consumer-oriented corporations have the same basic marketing needs. They need to increase traffic, increase sales, increase profits, project a positive public image, keep their employees happy, and document the effectiveness of their marketing dollars. By strengthening corporations' appeal with consumers, nonprofits help them do each of those things.

HOW NONPROFITS SHINE

Nonprofits Offer Corporations Instant Credibility.

Nonprofits are respected as experts in their field. Corporations can tap this expertise by developing joint ventures. When Levi Strauss wanted to promote its line of clothing for preschoolers, who better to work with than Bank Street College of Education, the nation's leader in early childhood education?

In a mutually beneficial joint venture, Levi's paid Bank Street to develop a booklet on hassle-free dressing for preschoolers. Levi's distributes the free booklet at point-of-purchase displays where customers buy toddlers jeans. Levi's gains credibility and sales. Bank Street gets its educational product paid for at a profit and distributed to a larger audience than it could ever reach on its own.

Nonprofits Help Corporations Reach Audiences They Might Never Reach On their Own.

Nonprofits have access to audiences that are closed to for-profit businesses. An appropriate, well-planned joint venture can help corporations access those markets.

Public schools are ordinarily closed to corporate advertising. But when a corporation sponsors visits by a Denver Children's Museum traveling exhibit, they are permitted to give a discount coupon to each student.

When B. Dalton Bookseller wanted to promote reading (and therefore book buying), they teamed up with the Public Broadcasting System (PBS) to create a four-year $3 million Literacy Initiative. Using marketing and community affairs money, Dalton funded the PBS series "Reading Rainbow." They also produced corollary materials for schools and libraries – places that their advertising dollars ordinarily could not reach.

Nonprofits Help Corporations Reach Targeted Audiences.

Frequently corporations want to reach specific audiences – people in a certain income bracket or with particular interests and lifestyles. An association with a nonprofit that serves that audience can help them do that.

When Post introduced its new Natural Raisin Bran cereal, they wanted to attract the attention of people given to a "natural" lifestyle. So they teamed up with the National Park Service. Over a three month period, they gave the Park Service a percentage of each Natural Raisin Bran sale.

Nonprofits Help Corporations Gain Positive Exposure In The Press.

Because they are unusual and positive in nature, joint ventures with nonprofits generally attract attention from the media. Corporations, rather than paying for advertising, find their ventures the subjects of features stories.

When Hallmark Cards promoted its Springbok jigsaw puzzles by sponsoring a jigsaw competition at the Dairy Barn, an arts center in Athens, Ohio, the contest was covered on the Today Show and in *Sports Illustrated*. Hallmark could not have purchased the positive public exposure with conventional advertising.

Advantages To A Nonprofit Are Many.

When a nonprofit joint ventures with a corporation, it suddenly packs the power, reach and financial clout of the corporation. From that special moment when the nonprofit changes its attitude toward itself and its approach to its goals, new fantasies begin to grow. The fantasies prompt strategies. Within months an enterprising nonprofit can be doing ventures that reach sizeable numbers of people and generate unrestricted income, money that can go toward operating expenses or to cover programs that won't pay for themselves. These are your "riches," controlled by you, not tied to funders' grant cycles or their priorities. The pace is predictable: you decide when and how many ventures you want to do.

Very quickly the nonprofit has three corporate pockets in which to dip. The two new ones, Marketing and Employee Relations, are larger and faster growing than the first. Funding options have increased rather than decreased. The nonprofit is more diversified and less vulnerable financially.

Now, instead of going to corporations for a contribution, hat in hand, nonprofits can come empowered with a business proposition. Building on their own strengths and expertise, entrepreneurial nonprofits can sell a product or service that meets a corporation's need. Unlike fundraising, this is an exchange of equal value, a business deal between partners in which both parties benefit. Not surprisingly, that is the definition of nonprofit enterprise.

PART II

Case Studies

Many nonprofits have begun doing this kind of "venturing" or "marketing." Some are big, multimillion dollar organizations that roll out national programs with major corporations. Others are small organizations with budgets of $50,000 working with a local retailer. Some are doing many projects at the same time and have started "enterprise divisions" within their organizations. Others are starting with one or two small projects and a long-term strategy. The scale of the projects is unimportant; the principles are the same. They should work for you regardless of the size of your organization, the field you're in, or your location. Here are two examples from very different organizations. What they have in common is enterprise spirit and success.

CHAPTER 5:

THE DENVER CHILDREN'S MUSEUM

The staff at the Denver Children's Museum likes to brag that the only Worker's Compensation claim it ever filed was when the Director of Public Relations wrenched her shoulder during a particularly rowdy game of nerf basketball in the office. Not absolutely true. The Museum's driver once hurt his back unloading a traveling exhibit. But that gives you an idea of the playful spirit and character of the Children's Museum.

If you walk into their landmark bright green building, then trot up to their third floor offices (topped by a purple pyramid familiar to most Denver families), it is easy to be deceived by the chaotic clutter of toys and exhibit pieces, and by the loud banter and laughter. It is easy to think there is not much work going on, and that a host of wealthy benefactors are to thank for this sunny, comfortable space. Not so. The clutter and laughter are actually the evidence of the hard work that is ongoing, while the new $3.2 million building is a testament to the success of the Museum's commitment to nonprofit enterprise.

BACKGROUND

The Museum's foray into enterprise began in 1977. After two itinerant "pilot" years, traveling to libraries and community centers, and three years in a dilapidated, 10,000 square foot former dairy, the Museum was virtually bankrupt. The three federal grants that made up the operating budget ended and no new money had been raised.

The Museum knew the ongoing problems with fundraising: the money was unpredictable, uncontrollable and slow; the Museum had no track record of success with which to impress a foundation; and the competition for grants was fierce. There had to be a better way to fund its operation. The surprise is that they decided to pursue larger, more flexible pools of money in the private sector. To do that the Children's Museum needed to convince businesses to invest in their mission.

They envisioned a museum that was funded by revenues from the sale of products and services to corporations. Those products and services would not only earn money; they would carry the Museum's message to a broad audience. Using this approach, they believed that the Museum could become self-sufficient and a national force in informal education. That vision became the driving force behind the Museum's operations.

The Museum knew, however, that if businesses were to purchase its products and services, they would have to get something in return. The Museum's products would have to meet business needs. How could a fledgling children's museum meet the needs of both itself and a business? That was the challenge.

VENTURES

Let's Go to the Mall

The Museum's first project was a traveling exhibit designed for shopping malls. Common sense told them that malls need to attract shoppers. Phone calls to several local mall managers told them that they spend money to do it. So the idea was hatched for a traveling Children's Museum exhibit on the arts. The exhibit would be participatory: it would give children a chance to experiment with music, fine art, dance and drama. Malls could rent the exhibit from Thursday through Sunday, advertise its presence, and attract families. At least, that was what the Children's Museum hoped.

They tested the idea on mall managers, and indeed, the managers were interested. Then with potential bookings set, the Museum used CETA (federal employment training) money to fund development and fabrication of the exhibit. *Voila*, Sensorium I was born – the Children's Museum's first earned income project!

Over its three year life, Sensorium made twenty-one visits to shopping malls. Each mall paid $1500 to host the exhibit for a four-day weekend. The Museum netted a total of $25,000.

Exploring the Book Biz

Buoyed by pleasant surprise, new found "riches," and that slightly rowdy spirit we alluded to earlier, the Museum took another step: a publication called *Denver City Games*. *City Games* was a book of activities that would encourage families to learn Denver history. Using a $2,300 foundation grant, the Museum wrote, designed and printed the book, then took it to local book stores. Several book stores were willing to carry it, in orders of five to seven copies at a time. That was obviously no way to move merchandise. It was slow and labor intensive.

Looking for a better way to sell large numbers of the book, the Museum asked itself a question that was to become the bedrock of its enterprise strategy: "Who needs or wants this item?"

Suddenly lights flashed; the answer came from nothing more than an openness to listen to any and all ideas. There it was: families who were new to Denver were a likely prospect. But how to reach them? Through the realtors who sold them houses. The Museum approached the Director of Marketing at a local real estate company and she bought 5,000 copies at a wholesale price. Simple, eh?

The Museum had stumbled on a strategic goldmine. In one sale they had sold bulk copies of the book, avoided any risk to themselves, and eliminated the need to spend hours looking for multiple buyers. They had discovered no-risk sales.

High on *City Games'* success, and using the same formula, they produced *A-Maze-ing Denver*, a book of pencil mazes of Denver landmarks which they sold to another real estate firm; *The Frontier Flying Fun Book*, a book on flight which they sold to Frontier Airlines; and *The Babysitter's Guide*, a guidebook on how to be a responsible babysitter which they sold to a bank, a home builder and a chain of day care centers for use as a re-enrollment incentive. The Museum had discovered the corporate use of premium items — inexpensive give-aways that businesses use to attract customers. Premiums became a staple of the Museum enterprise approach.

Extra! Extra!

Success has its privileges. For some time the Museum had been wanting to produce a newsletter for its growing family of members. Since it was a children's museum, the idea was to create a paper that would be mailed to the children in each family and contain activities and stories of interest to them. But the idea was stalled because the monthly printing and mailing costs would be too high for the organization's meager budget.

How could the idea of meeting business's needs be applied to the newsletter? Easy! Add advertising. But wait a minute, why would businesses want to advertise to the Museum's tiny, 500-family membership? Ad rates for that kind of circulation would never support the paper, much less bring a profit back to the Museum. Clearly, the circulation had to rise. Easy again with a little brainstorming! Distribute the paper in schools. Give a free copy to every kindergarten through sixth grade student in the six-county metro area, a circulation of 100,000. Advertisers love those big digits and they pay for them. So *Boing*! was born, the Children's Museum's newspaper, the third largest newspaper in the state of Colorado.

Schools liked *Boing*! because for them it was an innovative bi-monthly reading supplement that magnetized children on Friday afternoons. Advertisers liked it because for the first time they had access to the parents of school children. Restaurants, toy stores and other businesses that catered to families now had high visibility in their primary market. The advertisers put games, contests and discount coupons in their ads to measure response. They received favorable results. For the Museum, *Boing*! was both a "mission" and a marketing vehicle; it took the Museum's creative approach to education into thousands of homes that had never before heard of the Denver Children's Museum.

The staff of the paper was one full-time editor. She wrote most of the stories, recruited staff members to write others, and used the Museum's full-time artist for design, illustration and paste-up. Every other month they turned out an eight-page, tabloid-size paper that cost $6,000 to produce. Ad revenues per issue were $9,000, generating a bi-monthly profit of $3,000.

More Throttle

With the *Boing*! editor on staff full-time, the Museum became more sophisticated in its development and sale of publications. It developed an efficient system for producing profitable publications in which each book was sold twice. The first sale covered the writing, design and paste-up of the book. The second paid for its printing and distribution. The second sale was always to one or more corporations that used the publication as a premium item.

While the books were designed to be profitable, they also reflected the Museum's commitment to educational quality. Each book was activity-based. Each took a difficult subject and made it interesting and relevant to children. Each encouraged parent-child interaction. The books were designed to take the Museum's educational message to families who could never visit the center in person.

The publications system involved using the *Boing*! editor as manager, and then contracting with professionals for writing, design and production. This enabled the Museum to do more than one publication at a time, and to use a variety of writers and artists to create books with a variety of looks and copy styles. It meant the Museum could hire the top writers and artists in Denver because they were hired short-term, and their fees were written into the project budgets. The result was a series of exemplary publications that generated a high-quality image for the Museum and its corporate partners.

Pet Projects

The first publication to use the double-sale system was *Kids and Pets*, an activity book about caring for animals. The Museum was approached by the American Humane Association which was looking for a way to get its message into schools. Seeing the success of *Boing*! they felt the Museum could help. With $13,000 from the Humane Association, the Museum developed *Kids and Pets*. The money covered writing, design, illustration, production, Museum overhead (rent, phone, utilities, photocopy, insurance and a percentage of the editor's time, all cost out to the project) and a profit. What remained was to find a corporate partner to print the book and distribute it.

The standard, simple question had to be answered: what business would want . . . a booklet on pet care? Pet food companies, pet stores and/or manufacturers of pet products. With the book's mock-up in hand, the Museum approached several of each. After numerous phone calls and one false lead, they found a buyer: StarKist/9 Lives, pet food manufacturer. StarKist paid the Museum $1.25 per copy for 62,000 copies of *Kids and Pets*. They gave 12,000 to veterinarians, and used the remaining 50,000 as a premium, printing a coupon for it on their bags of cat food. Of the $1.25 per copy, 85 cents covered the cost of printing the book; the remainder was profit for the Museum.

The Museum next produced *Small Change*, a book on money and the economy. *Small Change* was produced for Citicorp which wanted a premium item to use in its Person-to-Person Financial Network. Citicorp paid the Museum a fee to develop and produce the book. They bought 60,000 copies in advance to use in attracting families to their centers. When a Citicorp banker took the book into his son's fifth grade class, the teacher's rave review sparked a second use. Citicorp purchased 250,000 additional copies to give to upper elementary classrooms in communities where it was building business. By reaching students they were reaching parents, Citicorp's target market.

Numerous publications followed. *Seldom Was Heard*, a look at the real history of the American West, was sold first to an insurance company which paid for writing, design and paste-up. The company gave copies to a local school district. Additional copies were bought by a local bank whose logo and advertising theme was "the pioneer spirit," and a local department store used it as a back-to-school give-away. The bank also gave copies to the local historic preservation organization which used the book as a membership incentive.

Your Children Our Children, booklets on problems facing America's children, was produced to accompany a PBS television series. Dayton Hudson Corporation contracted with the Museum to research and produce the guides, then gave them away to viewers who requested them. *After the Tears*, a book for parents of children with disabilities, was developed with money from the Colorado Department of Education. It was printed and distributed by several corporations as an employee benefit. Later it was sold to a commercial publishing house for national retail sale.

More Roadshows

During this same period, the Museum began to pursue a second area of earned income, traveling exhibits. Sensorium's success in shopping malls had hinted at the potential of that medium. Now the Museum wanted to test it further. The Museum bet that given the number of daily field trips to the Museum, schools just might be interested in an exhibit that could come to them.

Museum directors tested the idea on school principals at their monthly meeting in a nearby district. There the Museum directors described the exhibit they had in mind: "Colors To Go" would enable children in grades K-6 to experiment with basic principles of color mixing. It would accommodate one class at a time; it would fit in an empty classroom or on an auditorium stage; it would be set up and staffed by Museum personnel. Would the principals be interested in renting such an exhibit? If so, how long would they want it? How much would they pay? Much to the Museum's surprise every principal asked to rent it! The principals also offered suggestions on how to make it best meet their needs. Elated, the Museum directors took a bold step. They wrote dates on a piece of paper and circulated it around the room. How many principals would sign up for the exhibit now? When the paper returned, they had booked the as-yet-unbuilt exhibit into 23 schools.

The next step was to sell it to a corporation which would pay for its development and fabrication. With such strong interest from schools, the Museum approached Chevron Corporation. Chevron, wanting to build its public image, agreed to invest in the exhibit for $2,000. That tiny budget and Museum ingenuity created Colors To Go, the Children's Museum's first school-oriented traveling exhibit.

When set up, the exhibit filled a space 20' x 25', approximately the size of a school stage or empty classroom. Crated, it fit in the back of the Museum's panel truck. It could be set up and taken down in one hour by the Museum's driver, and could be used by every class in a school over a two- or three-day period. The Museum hired a contract "teacher" to accompany the exhibit on its bookings, paying the person only for hours worked. During its first year of life, Colors To Go visited 27 schools. Each one paid $165 a day. This fee covered the Museum's costs in operating and maintaining the exhibit, plus a profit.

After renting Colors To Go, schools clamored for more. Over the next several years, the Museum developed a fleet of traveling exhibits on subjects ranging from handicaps to everyday math. Each exhibit accommodated a classroom of children with a variety of participatory activities; each exhibit was accompanied by pre- and post-visit classroom materials, and each earned a profit on its $165/day rental fee. The Museum had discovered another winning formula.

As with publications, the formula included using a Museum staff person (the Director of Programs) as project manager, and hiring contract professionals for content expertise, design and fabrication. This enabled the Museum to produce more than one exhibit at a time, and to hire the specific skills it needed at an affordable cost. Concept and execution, likewise, were consistently fresh and diverse thanks to this approach.

As with the publications, the exhibit funding formula included selling the product twice. The initial sale was to a corporation that paid to produce the exhibit. Numerous companies that wanted to reach families paid the Museum an average of $18,000 to take their name into schools. That money covered the Museum's costs in producing the exhibits, plus a profit. The second "sale" was the rental which covered the exhibit's operating costs plus a profit.

While designed initially for schools, the exhibits were rented just as often by banks, shopping malls, family restaurants and other profit centers interested in attracting families. Even other children's museums became long-term exhibit renters. The Museum also rented the exhibits to businesses which would sponsor visits to schools in their neighborhoods. One business might sponsor an exhibit in three or four schools, enabling the Museum to make several sales with one phone call.

Special Events

The Museum's third major area of earned income activity was special events. These were events that created fun educational experiences for families at the same time that they provided targeted marketing opportunities for businesses.

The Museum's first special event was the Toy Trade, a pre-Christmas event designed to reinforce to children the importance of sharing with others. The event was held in a hotel ballroom; children brought old toys in good condition. One toy was given to charity, the others were traded for other children's old toys. Families went home with "new" old toys, and several Denver-area charities received a Christmas bounty. The event was based on the Museum's formula of "sharing, caring and greed." Museum staff knew that people like easy opportunities to demonstrate their caring and concern for people in need. They also knew that people like easy opportunities to share with those in need – as long as they walk away with something for themselves. An event that catered to those feelings was likely to be successful. The Toy Trade was.

A variety of corporations invested in the event. A real estate company, a fast food chain, a toy store and a department store each paid the Museum $2,300 to participate. For this fee, they became pre-event dropoff points for toys, distribution points for tickets, and were listed as Toy Trade partners in ads and statement stuffers which they produced. The Trade offered sponsors a way to increase their name visibility and build traffic. The association with a quality event and with a quality institution like the Children's Museum had great appeal to their largest markets. The Museum held the Toy Trade three consecutive years, selling it to three partners each year. The event's operating costs were $2,000, producing an annual net profit of $4,900. What's more, every event had a media partner, guaranteeing media coverage.

The Toy Trade was retired *before* decline set in. The Museum subscribes to the motto "quit on a high," which is good (if not always easy to follow) business sense.

Then they initiated the Parenting Fair. This was a trade show for new and expectant parents. Businesses serving that market bought booth space, demonstration times and program ads to advertise their products and services. Parents paid $4 at the door to get in, and spent hours stopping at booths, watching demonstrations, chatting with medical personnel and learning about parenting options. More sophisticated than the Toy Trade, and considerably larger in scope, the Parenting Fair cost $17,000 to produce. But its income was higher as well. Booths rented for $500, as did seminar and demonstration spaces. Program ads cost $800. "Sponsorship" of the event cost $2,500 and meant a company was included in all Parenting Fair literature and ads. Each year, the Fair netted the Museum approximately $25,000.

Again, as for traveling exhibits and publications, special events were engineered by one full-time staff person. The Museum's Director of Marketing sold the corporate sponsorships, arranged the event's programs, and hired contract professionals for graphics, construction, audio-visual, and other support services.

Special events are re-invented or retired by the fourth year.

SUCCESSFUL STRATEGIES

Over the years the Museum's projects became increasingly sophisticated. Their budgets increased, as did their revenues, and the number of projects surged. The Museum was on constant lookout for possible earned income opportunities, for possible match-ups between their own educational know-how and a company's marketing needs. How and where did it find them?

It found them by asking itself two questions:

1) "Who wants what we can do?" and

2) "What do businesses want?"

What We Can Do

"What we can do" referred to the Museum's wish list: exhibits, events and publications Museum staff felt were important based on their own research and knowledge of their audience. The Executive Director and Director of Marketing constantly looked for businesses that might want to buy those projects. Simultaneously, they examined the universe of businesses that, because they appealed to families, were potential business partners. They looked at banks, realtors, department stores and restaurants, and asked what could the Museum do for them? What kind of educational product or service would meet their needs?

The questions paid off. By 1983, five years after the self-sufficiency goal was set, the Museum was doing an average of fifteen earned income projects a year. They carried the Museum's educational vision across the country as well as across town, and generated approximately 95% of the Museum's income.

Principles to Live and Survive With

A set of principles undergird the financial success of the Children's Museum.

1) *PRE-SELLING* : The Museum never risks its own money in producing a product or event. It pre-sells all projects to corporate partners, and then uses that money to produce the project.

2) *WHOLESALING*: The Museum never sells retail to the general public. That way it never wonders how many sales it will make, and never sits on unsold inventory. Instead, it wholesales its products to a corporate partner, which, in turn, distributes them to its customers. The Museum makes one bulk sale for which it receives guaranteed cash.

3) *PRICING*: Prices for all Museum products and events include three components: the direct cost of producing the project, the indirect (or overhead) costs of producing the project, and a profit. Prices also include intangibles such as a perceived sense of fairness, competitiveness with comparable choices available and mutual satisfaction, sometimes called the greed factor.

4) *DIVERSIFICATION*: The Museum believes that income diversification is healthy and that no project should ever provide more than a quarter of the organization's budget. It pursues many projects at one time, scheduled, as much as possible, to provide a steady cash flow throughout the year.

5) *QUALITY*: Quality counts. The Museum's corporate partners respect Museum staff as experts in family education. That's why they agree to buy Museum products. Therefore they are not involved in project development. The Museum generally invites partners to look at a book or exhibit during development, but quality control rests strictly with the Museum.

Three More Success Factors

Three other factors contribute to the success of the Children's Museum earned income strategy.

Factor One: All Museum products and services meet specific partner needs. Malls rent traveling exhibits to build traffic. Retail businesses buy Museum publications which they use as premium items to increase sales. Businesses sponsor special events because they strengthen the businesses' public image. Corporations sponsor traveling exhibits in schools and malls because they give them visibility with families. In every case, the association with the Museum helps businesses appeal to their target market.

Factor Two: The Museum has a clear vision of itself as an entrepreneurial organization. This is critical to the development of Museum products and services. Since its earliest days, the Museum has defined itself as a maverick – as young and brash; as willing to take risks; as willing to make mistakes. Its small, energetic, like-minded staff has a decided bias for action. They have an exuberant, optimistic mindset – both educationally and financially. They believe learning is everywhere. They believe that what is important is less the subject and more the process by which learning happens. They love the challenge of matching a company's marketing needs with their own educational vision and expertise.

Factor Three: A broadly defined mission, purposely. Early on, the Museum decided that it was not just about exhibits for children. That is too narrow for an organization that believes learning has as much to do with self-worth as it does with content. In a world of falling test scores and families in crisis, the Museum believes that children everywhere need experiences of success. To provide those experiences, they have to reach parents. So the Museum takes its mission beyond its building to reach as many families as possible with experiences that promote self-esteem and family interaction. There is no question that this broad definition helps the Museum's marketing efforts. Any business that serves families is a potential partner, and a wide range of products and services are possible. All of them serve the Museum's mission to "provide high quality educational products and services for families."

MORAL DILEMMAS

Opportunism

The Denver Children's Museum's reliance on earned income requires that it be highly opportunistic. This opportunism occasionally prompts accusations: the Museum is asked if the "marketing tail" sometimes wags the "educational dog," if it does projects because of their financial gain rather than their educational benefit. Staffers say the Museum has never done a project with which it educationally disagrees, or with a partner it feels is inappropriate.

This is not to say that the Museum blindly accepts all partners. On the contrary, the programs staff takes seriously its responsibility to challenge any project which it feels is inappropriate. It has done this three times.

The first time concerned an advertiser in *Boing*! Several issues in a row, the back page ad in *Boing*! was purchased by Pepsi. Programs staff protested. They felt soft drinks were not healthy for children, and that it was inappropriate for the Children's Museum to promote them.

Marketing staff countered that children see soft drink ads in many places and are fed soft drinks by their parents. The placement of a Pepsi ad in *Boing*! would not prompt children to drink it, any more than eliminating the ad would discourage them from doing so. If programs staff wanted to encourage children to examine the health risks of soft drinks, they could do so more effectively with an article in a future issue. More important, the marketers felt, was that the guaranteed income from the series of ads made publication of future issues possible. The decision was left to the Directors of Marketing and Programs, who decided to keep the ads.

The issue raised a serious moral dilemma inherent to nonprofit enterprise. Key to the enterprise system is the relationship between the nonprofit and its corporate partners. Are there potential partners that a nonprofit should avoid? Clearly the answer is yes. Less clear, is how to determine which ones. For the Museum the answer came by weighing the pros and cons. While Pepsi was deemed OK, other advertisers were later rejected. The Museum developed no hard and fast criteria for determining partner suitability, preferring to examine each case individually. "Every organization must find its own bottom line," says the Museum's former marketing director. "You have to weigh your image, your constituents, and the goals of the project, and trust your gut about whether a corporation is right for you."

Partner Input

The second challenge to the Museum's educational integrity came when the Museum produced *Small Change* for Citicorp. As part of the agreement, Citicorp asked to review the book at various stages of development. The Museum agreed. No previous partners had ever asked for changes or input; the review was merely a courtesy. To the staff's surprise, at the first review, Citicorp challenged some of the material. They felt the Museum had not explained banking adequately. Staff countered that the purpose of the book was not to explain banking, but to explain the function of money in a complex system of which banking was just one part.

After several discussions an agreement was reached. The role of banking would be limited to what the staff felt was appropriate, but Citicorp would continue to review the publication for economic accuracy. Unfortunately, every subsequent review prompted similar debates. These slowed the process, the book missed its deadline by several months, and the staff, not surprisingly, grumbled.

Once the book was out, however, and tempers had cooled, the staff willingly admitted that the process had produced a better book. The input of the corporation, while annoying, had in fact, pushed them to find ways to explain economic complexities in children's terms. Left on their own, they would have made the book simpler than it had to be.

This issue raised a different moral dilemma for the Museum. This was the first time a partner had demanded input on a project. How far could the Museum bend to accommodate its wishes? What they found was that by educating the partner and sticking to their guns, they didn't need to bend at all. They were able to accept suggestions they felt were appropriate, and reject those they disagreed with. The incident reinforced the importance of guarding their educational integrity, at the same time that it taught them valuable skills for working with partners.

Stretching Your Mission

The third challenge came when the Museum agreed, with some trepidation, to produce an exhibit for a sheep producers association. What educational message could they derive from sheep? They decided to include activities about sheep shearing and the process of turning raw wool into finished fabric. Families enjoyed the completed exhibit but Museum staff felt uncomfortable with it. For the first time they felt they had overstepped the bounds of educational validity. The exhibit wasn't bad, but it was on a subject that didn't merit the time and attention spent. Given the opportunity cost of every project, what other exhibit hadn't they done, because of doing this one?

The episode taught them an important lesson. By overstepping the bounds this once, they protected themselves from doing it again. The project made them more careful about which partners to work with, and about trusting their educational intuition about how far to stretch for a partnership.

The Museum minimizes its need to stretch by making its "marketing bottom line" an educational one. Programs Department staff are the quality conscience for the institution and projects are not undertaken without their approval. This naturally produces tensions between marketing and programs staffs. But the Museum finds these tensions healthy because they force constant examination and re-evaluation of goals. They promote the ongoing questioning of assumptions which is a hallmark of Children's Museum operations.

LESSONS LEARNED

The Museum's earned income strategy has produced numerous benefits in addition to money.

- **Market-orientation has required the Museum to be extremely responsive to its customers.** It stays in close touch with the changing needs of children, families and the people who serve them in order to deliver products and services that are on target.
- **Diversity and impatience have accelerated staff learning.** The Museum's emphasis on diversity coupled with its staff's impatience has prompted it to do many projects in a short period of time. This has enabled the staff to learn quickly about what works and what doesn't. Each project's experience is quickly incorporated into the next, which accounts in part, for the rapid growth in sophistication of Museum projects.
- **Corporate partners have helped disseminate the Museum's message to a broader audience than it would ever have reached on its own.** Broad distribution and the quality required to make it work, enabled the Museum to grow in five years from a sleepy exhibit center serving 10,000 people annually to a national organization reaching millions of families.

Traditional Fundraising

Until recently the Children's Museum had done little traditional fundraising. Foundation grants were used primarily as seed money for earned income products. The Museum never did a phone or direct mail campaign. Until the capital campaign for the new building, it didn't even have a Development Committee on the board. (Even the Museum's membership program operated as an earned income venture: the Museum packaged memberships as corporate premium items and sold them wholesale to day care chains, toy stores, dentists, professionals, and other businesses that gave them away to families.)

Since 1984, with increased operating costs in the new building, a new director, and a depressed Denver economy, the Museum has eased its adamant self-sufficiency stance. Fundraising now contributes 12% of its $1.2 million budget. Still, "educational enterprise" is the major thrust of the Museum's operations, outlook and budget. Under director Alby Segal, the Museum is – if anything – pursuing larger, more ambitious projects. Segal is positioning the Museum as an "educational think tank" for corporate America. It is undertaking development and design of large scale projects outside the Museum, and using those projects to support Museum operations.

NEWEST EXPERIMENTS

Positioning a Ski Resort

In one project, the Museum has contracted with Vail Associates to develop a children's center at Vail ski resort. Vail wants to position itself as the ski area for families, and they know the Children's Museum is the perfect partner to help them.

Satellite Museums

The Museum has contracted with a local McDonald's franchisee to put small-scale children's museums in three McDonald's restaurants. If the centers are successful, the Museum will develop a customized catalog of participatory educational exhibits for purchase by McDonald's franchisees nationally. The Museum has also contracted with Denver's Stapleton International Airport and American Express to put a satellite children's museum at the airport.

Trick or Treat Street

In another project, the Museum is taking a good idea national. For several years at Halloween, the Museum has run Trick or Treat Street, a safe alternative to trick or treating. Corporate sponsors buy store fronts on the fabricated city street and give away educational materials and healthy snacks. Thousands of families pay $2 at the door, and between their fees and store front sponsorships, the Museum nets approximately $25,000 each year.

In 1989, Trick or Treat Street will go national. For an annual franchise fee, the Museum has sold the rights to the event to a national fast food corporation. The corporation will arrange with malls and nonprofit organizations in three cities to host the event, and will pay the Museum a consulting fee to teach the local hosts how to run it. They will pay an additional one-time fee for the creation of a Trick or Treat Street guide book.

That the Museum is able to implement these ventures with a new director, new staff, higher operating costs and a depressed local economy is testimony to the strength of the enterprise concept. While many factors have changed, the essential ones remain the same. The Museum is committed to first class quality in everything it does. It is action-oriented and willing to take risks. It is constantly looking for opportunities to match its educational capabilities with a corporation's needs. The Museum subscribes to an entrepreneurial vision in which earned income is a means of delivering its educational mission. Through its attitudes and behaviors, the Museum makes that vision real; it lives it.

CHAPTER 6:

The National Crime Prevention Council

At the National Crime Prevention Council, enterprise has taken a different route. Rather than pursuing many small projects with a wide variety of corporate partners — as the Denver Children's Museum chose to do — NCPC has developed a small number of partnerships, each of which has produced a large, lucrative, ongoing campaign.

NCPC chooses its partners carefully. It works closely with them to develop both parties' needs. By producing high quality materials, it has turned each partnership into a long-lasting, mutually beneficial relationship. To NCPC, enterprise is not just a means of generating income. It is a primary means of spreading the crime prevention message.

BACKGROUND

NCPC was formed in 1982 to serve as the focal point of a national crime prevention campaign whose leading symbol was McGruff, the crime dog. The council receives core funding from the U.S. Department of Justice (Office of Justice Programs) and works in partnership with the Advertising Council (the nonprofit arm of the advertising industry) and the National Crime Prevention Coalition (118 state and national organizations) to develop educational materials, distribute them to millions of Americans, and help America "take a bite out of crime."

VENTURES

A few years ago NCPC realized the power of national corporations for reaching large numbers of people. With local customer bases and national advertising networks in place, businesses were perfectly positioned to help them spread the crime prevention message.

Going Local Nationally

For their first partnership they approached Southland Corporation, owner of 7-11 Stores. Southland was a calculated choice as 7-11 Stores are frequently victims of crime, and Southland had already targeted crime as an issue of corporate concern. They had recently implemented an internal crime prevention campaign and had developed ties with local crime prevention agencies and neighborhood groups.

In 1981 NCPC approached Southland to become their partners in crime prevention by putting McGruff posters and brochures in their stores. Southland agreed. This was a perfect fit with Southland's own marketing and image goals: it positioned them as "a neighborhood store," concerned with the safety of its customers.

Customers responded. In the first two years of the campaign they picked up 20 million McGruff brochures from 7-11's front counters. NCPC and Southland knew they were on to something. NCPC had found a powerful vehicle for spreading its message; Southland had found an effective means of reaching millions of customers with a "we care" message. The two organizations decided to increase the level of partnership.

Safe at Home

NCPC's second corporate partnership was with Texize Division of Dow Consumer Products, manufacturer of household cleaners. Like Southland, Texize was already involved in crime prevention. With products geared to families, they had targeted the area of children's safety; they were interested in a national effort to teach parents and children about self-protection.

In 1985, with this in mind, Texize approached NCPC. The Council helped them produce a *Children's Emergency Phone Book*, a booklet on protecting yourself when home alone. Texize offered the booklet free with proof-of-purchase seals. In a companion drive, Texize offered to make a donation to NCPC for every customer coupon redeemed during a specified period. The result: 500,000 *Emergency Phone Books* were distributed. What's more, Texize sold a lot of product and NCPC earned $50,000 from the coupon drive while reaching thousands of families with important information. The two organizations were ready for a second, larger, partnership.

Safe at School

Their second effort was Kidsmart, a multi-faceted campaign which used McGruff to carry the safety message to schools. NCPC had developed a McGruff Drug Prevention and Personal Protection curriculum for elementary grades. The curriculum contained a McGruff hand puppet and a set of audio tapes which teach children proper safety behaviors. Through a special dealer incentive program, Texize offered to distribute the curriculums.

In national media Texize advertised that for every 200 cases of Texize products ordered by a store, the company would donate a one-grade McGruff curriculum package to a school of the retailer's choice. For every 1000 cases bought, they would donate a curriculum for the entire school.

Texize also made a shortened version of the curriculum available to parents as a self-liquidating premium. They purchased McGruff hand puppets and audio tapes from NCPC, and advertised that for $4.99 plus one proof-of-purchase seal from any Texize product. In this way, Texize recouped its cost of purchasing the packages from NCPC, and parents got puppet/cassette packages for teaching safety lessons at home. In a simultaneous national consumer coupon drive, Texize also donated 20 cents to NCPC for every coupon redeemed.

The results of the campaign were staggering. NCPC received over $200,000 in donations. Families wanting McGruff curriculums in their schools and homes gave Texize its strongest sales quarter ever. At the same time, NCPC reached millions of children and families with a strong crime prevention message.

MORAL DILEMMAS

Implied Endorsements

Another NCPC corporate partner is ADT, manufacturer of security systems. The Council had targeted rising workplace crime as an important area of attack. They needed a corporation to fund the development of educational materials and help distribute them. ADT, already in the workplace crime prevention business, was a natural choice. So NCPC asked them to fund development and production of a Corporate Action Kit. The kit would contain reproducible materials on protecting children at home alone, on drug and alcohol abuse, on street safety, and on other areas of crime prevention.

ADT agreed, and purchased 20,000 copies of the Kit for use as a premium item. ADT distributes the kits through its sales force. This strengthens customer contacts and builds company recognition for ADT's local offices. Through the partnership, NCPC reaches hundreds of thousands of workers with valuable crime prevention suggestions. They also reach many new corporations, each of whom is a potential partner.

The partnership also raised an important philosophical question for NCPC. McGruff's mandate was to fight crime. If he was to maintain his integrity, as well as his government funding and Ad Council support, he had to steer clear of product endorsement. Could NCPC work with a manufacturer of security systems and avoid implicitly endorsing their products? Furthermore, how closely can NCPC work with any corporation without seeming to endorse it?

The question is an important one that goes right to the heart of the partnership system. It is one the Council still discusses, in an ever-vigilant effort to maintain integrity. They feel that their role, and McGruff's, is to talk about crime, not about alarms or other corporate products. As long as they hold to that firm guideline, they can steer clear of implied endorsements. They followed that line in the development of the Corporate Action Kit: in the entire kit, security devices are mentioned only once. On a checklist for safeguarding your home is the suggestion that you "consider installing a security device." ADT and NCPC were both happy with the careful wording.

To prevent misuse from occurring in the future, the Council established a Quality Review Committee which meets weekly to review all uses of McGruff for accuracy of information and possible implicit endorsements.

The popularity of the McGruff symbol and its potential for misuse have made NCPC realize that they have to be extremely careful in choosing partners. "We realize that partners who gain corporate as well as community benefit are more likely to be long-term allies. The key is to choose companies wise enough to balance the two," says Allie Bird, Director of the Department of Corporate Initiatives. "It is essential that they understand our message and that that we understand theirs."

Thus, NCPC has learned to scrutinize potential partners carefully. They choose partners already active in public service so the partnership is a natural fit with the company's existing objectives. Both partners talk openly about their goals.

"People are driven by visions of things they want," says Allie. "You have to explore your visions together and find a venture in which they mesh."

Sticking to Priorities

A second philosophical question arose in 1986. The Council was approached by MasterCard. Impressed by the quality and breadth of NCPC materials, MasterCard wanted to develop a joint national campaign against credit card fraud. NCPC agreed, and together the organizations produced a package of materials for banks and retail merchants.

The package included a McGruff poster on five ways to prevent credit card fraud; a statement stuffer on how to protect your cards; and a merchants' brochure and videotape on how to detect fraud and prevent it. MasterCard sold the packages inexpensively to banks and retail merchants, where they became a hot item.

Impressed with the success of the campaign, MasterCard wanted to do a second partnership. They hoped to extend the fraud campaign with a Spanish language version of the materials. NCPC was reluctant. While an important issue, credit card fraud was not on their agenda for a major campaign. They were more concerned with rising crime on college campuses.

The two organizations negotiated their divergent needs and reached a compromise. They would do the fraud campaign extension. This would include a MasterCard sponsorship of McGruff posters for mass transit which would strengthen NCPC's public identity. Immediately following, MasterCard would underwrite development of materials for the college market.

For the first time NCPC had been asked to create a campaign that was not their own priority. They had successfully negotiated a compromise that met both partners' goals, but would they always be able to do that? If not, how far could they deviate from their own goals in order to develop corporate partners? The answer, they decided, is to be very clear about their own priorities, to continually evaluate them, and to choose partners whose marketing goals mesh with their own. At the same time they have to be flexible. Enterprise is not a game with rigid rules; each partnership has to be individually negotiated. The Council trusts its integrity and commitment to its mission. They trust themselves to make the right decision.

SUCCESSFUL STRATEGIES

It's easy to erroneously attribute NCPC's success to their sheer size, national presence, and government and Ad Council support. While those assets help them implement campaigns, they don't help them chart the overall direction that Council activities follow. Rather, it is attitudes of key staff that account for NCPC's enterprise success. Primary are their willingness to be flexible and their market orientation. These two qualities have enabled NCPC to see opportunities for partnerships and to grab them.

Re-examining Our Mission

From its earliest days, NCPC defined its mission broadly. They believe crime stems from the unraveling of community and the resulting lack of control people feel. Prevention means ending isolation, creating positive role models, and mending broken family and community ties. Defining their mission this broadly has several advantages. It enables NCPC to attack the problem comprehensively, and opens many avenues for programs. Seniors, teenagers, children, crime on college campuses, crime in the workplace, child abuse, drug and alcohol abuse: each becomes a focus for a crime-prevention campaign. Each also opens the door for corporate partners. As NCPC addresses the needs of specific markets, they have something to offer corporations that also serve those markets.

The list of audiences – and partners – is constantly growing as NCPC researches changing needs. Their attentiveness to the market, their recognition of changing needs, and their eagerness to seek opportunities and act on them has made NCPC extremely effective at meeting its mission *and* generating revenue.

Dividing the Workload

Remarkably, this range of partnerships has been designed and directed by primarily three people. Jack Calhoun, NCPC's Executive Director, Mac Gray, Director of Marketing and Special Projects, and Allie Bird, until recently, Director of Program Development are the primary sales, management and creative team. Together they bring a comprehensive perspective to each venture. As they challenge each others' thinking, ventures are thoroughly analyzed before implementation.

How are three people able to handle these projects in addition to their regular work of running the Council? Actual implementation of the campaigns is handled by contract specialists. As at the Denver Children's Museum, the use of paid staff as managers and contract staff as implementers, greatly increases the resources of the Council. It provides a wide variety of skills, spreads management over many projects, and makes possible multiple campaigns that are high quality and affordable. It also enables the Council to streamline its operation. The small number of key players, the sympatico nature of their thinking, and their power in making decisions, makes NCPC fast and efficient. They can act quickly on market opportunities, work on their partners' time schedules, and make rapid mid-course corrections. As Allie Bird says, "We have an amazing balance of consensus and fast-tracking."

Much of the work is done by NCPC's partners. Once the two organizations have defined the goals and parameters of a campaign, NCPC trusts its partners to develop materials. They guide the process and review all materials before publication. This extends the Council's resources, and enables them to take advantage of the professional skills of their partners. NCPC also draws on internal resources. Within the Council different departments handle specific areas of crime prevention. Their skills and expertise are "hired" when they apply to a particular project.

The Council has systematized enterprise over the years. Recently, they created a separate department for handling partnerships, the Department of Corporate Initiatives, with Allie as Director and a staff of four. This reflects the importance of partnerships to NCPC, and their dedication of resources to the program. The Executive Director and Marketing Director, who are not in the new department, will continue to play vital roles in partnership development, and Allie will continue to do fundraising and program development outside of partnerships. As with its work with individual partners, NCPC recognizes the need to be clear, but flexible, in its internal structuring.

The Corporate Partnership System

Corporate partnership at NCPC continues to grow; its hallmark remains the close affinity between the Council and its partners. What makes these partnerships so successful?

• **Fundamental to the partnership concept is corporate "ownership" of the campaign and its message.** NCPC's partners don't just buy a marketing campaign. They buy *into* a crime prevention strategy for America. They adopt the crime prevention issue as part of their corporate identity. They enjoy the feeling that not only are they looking good to customers, they are *doing* good for their country and their communities.

• **NCPC promotes this ownership in several ways.**

l) **They choose partners who are already interested in public service.** This way they don't have to convince corporations of the importance of social action. By aligning their programs with a company's existing marketing goals, they integrate "doing good" into "doing good business."

2) **They work very hard to learn and meet their partners' needs.** As much as possible, NCPC materials and programs help partners build traffic, visibility and sales, and provide benefits for employees. They also promote good community relations on the national and local levels. While working with the national office of each corporation, they develop variations that can be implemented by local branches.

3) **They work closely with each partner to develop the campaign.** NCPC knows that people feel strongly about things they've had a hand in creating. At the same time, they need to protect the quality and integrity of the content. That can be a tricky balancing act. "In the beginning," says Allie Bird, "you have to get your mission embedded in your partners' minds. You have to set the parameters of the project — what you will and will not do — and then you have to trust them." This accomplished, campaigns are developed jointly, each partner respecting the other's expertise. Both parties approve final content. NCPC, supremely committed to excellence, zealously guards the integrity of its products.

4) **They make the campaign an integral part of their partner's business.** By involving many facets of their business in it, they give multiple layers of the company a chance to get involved and a chance to benefit. For instance, when Texize promoted McGruff Safety Curriculums, the promotion involved Texize mass retailers (who sold additional product), and Texize customers (who were given the opportunity to benefit NCPC by redeeming coupons and benefit their schools by buying Texize products).

5) **They give partners room for creativity in the implementation of the campaign on the local level.** During the Texize campaign, one of Texize's major retailers, Wal-Mart Stores, developed a promotion of its own. Local Wal-Mart Stores organized fundraisers to purchase additional safety curriculums for their schools. By matching each community's contribution, the Wal-Mart Foundation donated $50,000 toward curriculum purchases.

6) **They consistently produce high quality materials.** Corporations are impressed by the quality of NCPC's past campaigns, and are rewarded with equally impressive campaigns of their own. NCPC uses the best designers, advertising people, copywriters, video producers and crime prevention people in the field. They are willing to pay top dollar when necessary because the professional fees are built into their corporate partners' fees. They see themselves as the Top Dog in the crime prevention field and everything they do reflects that image. Their corporate partners are proud to have that quality and image working for them.

LESSONS LEARNED

• **Don't undervalue your worth.** The relationship with MasterCard produced another valuable lesson for NCPC. They realized they had been underpricing their partnerships. For as little as $1000, they had been selling their credibility and expertise to businesses that routinely spent many times that on advertising campaigns that couldn't match a partnership for marketing power. So in 1986 the Council created the Corporate Partnership Program. Twenty-four corporations have signed on as Charter Gold Members. Each has paid NCPC $10,000 for the privilege of working with them to develop a customized campaign that meets both parties' needs.

They have also introduced $25,000 partnerships with their old friends at Texize and Southland. The new Texize campaign will focus on drug abuse, a high priority for both organizations. It will include school kits, computer games and video tapes that use McGruff to help kids say no to drugs. The new Southland campaign will include a major McGruff campaign in 7-11 Stores nationwide.

The issue of pricing partnerships fairly is an ongoing one. As with every aspect of nonprofit enterprise, there is no steadfast formula. NCPC continues to experiment with new partnerships and pricing strategies, but they've learned not to undervalue their worth.

• **Help your partners believe your message.** Every corporate contact is a chance for NCPC to teach its partners about crime prevention and the NCPC message. Whether discussing a major campaign, approving an ad, or merely have lunch, every conversation is an opportunity to show partners a new angle on the mission. NCPC staff ask their partners a lot of questions. They become familiar with their business. They learn about their personal lives. They look for ways to make crime prevention touch their partners' hearts. The result: emotional investment. NCPC partners come back for more. Many continue crime prevention initiatives on their own. Many bring their business partners into a campaign. This makes for successful ventures and it extends NCPC's resources. As their partners take up the cause, they carry the NCPC message farther than the Council ever could on its own.

Most partnerships don't start at this advanced level. They start with one small venture and grow as partners learn more about each other. NCPC has found that relationships built solely on meeting business needs do not work as well or last as long as those in which both partners believe in the mission. Once that is achieved, the ongoing investment of time pays off repeatedly.

The National Crime Prevention Council has developed its own brand of nonprofit enterprise. Like the organization it serves, it is growing and changing. For Council partners, it is a powerful marketing mechanism; for the Council, it provides significant revenue and a potent tool for meeting its mission. NCPC partnerships are true win/win situations.

Vision: Creating the Fantasy

Developing An Entrepreneurial Vision

"Show me a man with both feet on the ground and I'll
show you a man who can't put his pants on."
— Arthur K. Watson

Now it's time to roll the dice — to use the theory we gave you in Part I and the case studies we gave you in Part II to form your own enterprising vision. The following exercises are launch pads for meshing enterprise with your organization's goals. Remember as you do them: enterprise isn't just a means of making money. It's a way of thinking and operating your entire organization.

DO YOU WANT A DATE WITH ENTERPRISE?

If you're courting enterprise, be advised: it's both visible and invisible. It's visible because the ventures you choose are there for all to see; because your partners reflect you; because your relationship shows on your bottom line. But underlying these outer signs is a holistic vision of what the organization can do and be. Entrepreneurial nonprofits embrace visions in which enterprise is a vital part of achieving their missions. The vision is a living, breathing definition of what the organization does, who it does it for, and how it does it. The vision is cultivated by management; actively shared with staff, board and public, and is reflected in everything the organization does. For this reason, entrepreneurial nonprofits don't do isolated income ventures. Each venture is part of the vision, one more step in accomplishing the mission.

THE FIRST TEMPTATION OF NONPROFITS

Forget about flirting with enterprise. It's tempting to do a venture or two and say, "If these work, we'll do more." But that's dangerous. The ventures become simply vehicles for making money. You lose the holistic vision in which ventures become vital to meeting your goals.

This all-or-nothing commitment will make some of you anxious, especially in a society where a half hour of concentration is frequently 30 minutes too long and where everyone wants guarantees though none can ever be practical. But you'll find the long-term benefits of "marriage" outlast the short-term attraction of quickie encounters.

Enterprise requires a long-term commitment.

PICTURE A THREE-YEAR COURTSHIP

Your vision is a concrete picture of where you want your organization to be in three years. No more, no less. It is a countdown, a goal you will work toward, broken into achievable pieces. Make it firm, make it measurable. We will show you how in subsequent chapters. Your vision is a series of pictures – both verbal and pictoral – that describe every aspect of your operation. John Sculley of Apple Computers said, "The best way to predict the future is to invent it." Forming a vision is your chance to do that.

In the process of developing your vision, you have to dream a bit. Put away this morning's memos. Put away every assumption about how your organization operates. You're creating a new organization. For now, anything is possible!

We are not suggesting you create an unachievable vision. Just the opposite! Visions are inspiring because they *are* achievable. Think big, create lofty goals: then break them down into smaller, more manageable steps that you can see yourself accomplishing. Your staff and the public will get excited because they can envision success.

EN-VISION THE FANTASY

Creating a vision is a systematic process. It requires questioning, brainstorming and gathering information – from inside and outside your organization. You will examine your strengths and expertise. You will study the audiences you serve and the trends that affect them. You will ask "Who needs or wants what we can do?" and, "What can we do for others?

You will translate this information into a statement and pictures that communicate to your staff, to your public and to your funders, the direction you are headed and the dynamism with which you'll get there.

THE ENTERPRISE CHAMPION

To guide this process, you'll need an Enterprise Champion, someone on staff who understands the concept, believes in enterprise for your organization, who can make it happen. This may be your executive director or CEO, it may be a top manager. Whoever it is must be given the time and responsibility to implement the necessary changes, and the power to make them happen.

The Enterprise Champion must be free to focus on enterprise development. This is serious business: not unusually difficult but requiring time, commitment and nurturing. Do not hamper your EC by expecting shortcuts.

You'll also need an Enterprise Champion on your board. Once again, it must be someone who understands the concept and believes in it for the organization; someone who can make it happen. Choose someone persuasive who can influence trustees who may be reluctant to try a new direction.

THE ENTERPRISE TEAM

Start the process by creating an Enterprise Team. This should include two key staff, two key board members (including, of course, your two Enterprise Champions) and a business person who is not a board member. The team will meet several times over the next three or four weeks to do the exercises on the following pages. If possible, hold the meetings away from the office — away from telephones, crises, interruptions. Keep meetings under two hours. That gives you time to warm up, roll, and quit on a high. Beyond that, people's energy starts to decline.

The process should be fun, exciting, energizing and team building. Share the experience with the rest of the staff. Talk about the process at board meetings. Let the spirit and the laughter of your meetings infuse your new entrepreneurial vision.

CHAPTER 8:

Asking Questions: A Starting Point

"As you may know, I have many good friends in the press who, unfortunately, have thus far refused to identify themselves and go public."
—Frank Sinatra,
White House connection

Exercise: An Organizational Questionnaire

Why do it?

What do people *really* feel about you and your organization? The following questionnaire is designed to elicit information about your organization from a variety of people: insiders who know you well; outsiders who know you through direct contact; even outsiders who know you solely by reputation.

The questionnaire asks for honest comments on various aspects of the organization. In doing so, it gives people a chance to be creative — to offer their best suggestions for strengthening your operation. It offers them a chance to be critical — to voice the concerns they might not otherwise offer. And it gives them a chance to feel involved — to contribute to your organization.

Their viewpoints should provide concrete suggestions for new programs and directions, as well as insights that you are too close to see. You may not always like what you hear, but if you *use* the information, any short-term discomfort should be offset by important long-term gains.

What to do:

Administer the questionnaire to two or three people in *each* of the following categories:

- STAFF — key decision makers
- BOARD MEMBERS — those with the greatest influence over the organization
- BOOSTERS — staunch supporters of your organization
- SKEPTICS — persistent skeptics or opponents of your organization
- COMPETITORS — your organization has them

- FOUNDATIONS OR CORPORATIONS – who have given you money
- FOUNDATIONS OR CORPORATIONS – who have declined to give you money
- EXPERTS OR "GURUS" – in your field
- RECIPIENTS – of your services
- OPINION LEADERS – progressive members of your community

> *"Bad alibi like dead fish – cannot stand test of time."*
> –Charlie Chan,
> *master detective*

Don't prejudice the answers you gather. To get honest answers you will have to assure confidentiality, so hire someone to ask the questions for you. Pick someone who is a good listener, sincere, and not connected with your organization. Have him or her conduct the interviews in person whenever possible. Most interviews should take 20 or 30 minutes. Assure each interviewee that completed questionnaires will not be shown to the organization. Instead, have the interviewer present you with the list of questions, each question followed by all the answers given to it. While interviewee's names should be excluded, they should be grouped into two categories: staff and board, and everyone else.

QUESTIONNAIRE

1. What will this organization will be like in five years?

   What *should* it be like?

2. What will it be like in the year 2000?

   What *should* it be like?

3. What are the organization's top three assets?

4. What are its top three limitations?

5. What three adjectives describe this organization best?

6. Ideally, what should a marketing plan for this organization include?

   What should it not include?

7. Once a marketing plan is completed, what three factors in the organization will help it get implemented?

   What three factors will hinder its implementation?

8. What are the "sacred cows" in the organization, the areas no one can touch or change or talk about?

9. What organizations (for-profit and/or nonprofit) do you most admire, and why?

What organizations do you least admire, and why?

10. Is there anything you'd like to add?

* * *

Using the Information:

In evaluating the questionnaire, look for consistency in the answers.

- **Do insiders and outsiders say the same things?** Outsiders may be more accurate since they are not biased by closeness.

- **Note the adjectives people use** to describe you, your staff and most of all your organization. The adjectives will help you define operating goals worth working toward and may suggest new products and services.

- **Does your organization have the characteristics of an entrepreneurial nonprofit?** Or are there areas you need to work on?

- **Is your organization capable of moving quickly on an idea?** Once you've developed a marketing plan, will you be able to act on it with speed? Or do you have organizational hurdles you first need to clear?

- **Look for potential earned income ventures** in the suggestions for an "ideal marketing plan" (Question #6).

- **Evaluate your interviewees**, using responses to Question #9. What kinds of organizations do they admire? Progressive, entrepreneurial ones whose examples you want to follow? Or organizations following a conventional path? Knowing this can help put their other comments in perspective.

You won't agree with every response, but you should take every one seriously. People's perceptions are real to them, even if you think they're inaccurate. Use the answers to show yourself where your organization needs to change. This gathering of information could be one of the most revealing and valuable exercises you'll do for your organization.

"The pure and simple truth
is rarely pure and never simple."
—Oscar Wilde,
author/playwright

CHAPTER 9:

Evaluating Your Style

"I thought Brian was a perfect gentleman, apart from
buttering his head and trying to put it between two
slices of bread."
—Tom Petty, The Heartbreaker,
assessing Brian Wilson, The Beach Boy,
at a Los Angeles restaurant

Exercise: List your operating characteristics

Why do it?

When you administered the questionnaire in the last chapter, you found a list of adjectives people used to describe your organization. Some were flattering; others may have been a bit messy, or worse. Taken together, the adjectives probably paint a realistic portrait of how your organization operates. Listing them lets you examine the portrait to decide which parts you like and which parts you'd like to change. (Hiding them under cosmetics won't do either, you'll end up looking like Tammy Faye Bakker, and you'll cry alone.)

In this exercise you'll take the list one step further. You will list adjectives that you want to describe your organization in the future. This second list will give you operating goals to work toward.

What to do:

1. Call a one hour meeting of the Enterprise Team. Using a blackboard or large newsprint pad, make a list of all the adjectives (or phrases) you can think of that describe your organization. Start with the ones from the organizational questionnaire, then add others. Don't forget, accurate adjectives can sting a little too.

2. When you finish the list, think ahead to the future. Suppose you could "fix" the organization in the next three years. What adjectives would describe you then? Make a second list of those.

3. Tell the Team the following story. It will help them get started:

The Canadian National Institute for the Blind provides support services to the visually impaired, and handicap awareness education for the general public. They made the following two lists to describe their organization.

Current year adjectives:

respected	sense of humor
cautious	stodgy
underutilized	not well enough known
old fashioned	approachable
qualified	slow-moving
entrenched	reluctant to change
bureaucratic	

Future fantasy adjectives:

dynamic	respected (by handicapped)
profitable	respected (by general public)
flexible	creative
innovative	experimental
heavily-used	loved
efficient	more streamlined
visionary	

Developing the lists helped CNIB in two ways. It forced them to pinpoint operating characteristics of their organization, although they didn't always like what they saw. It made them think about how they *want* to operate. By listing adjectives for the future, they created operating goals to work toward.

Using the Information:

The future qualities you have ascribed to your organization will be incorporated into your entrepreneurial vision. Over the next few exercises, the vision will become clearer, as will the path for getting there.

CHAPTER 10:

What Are Your Assets?

"In ancient times, wealth was expressed in many forms. A man might be judged by his sheep herds, dog packs or assets."
— Luke Deepur,
mime interpreter

Exercise: List your tangible and intangible assets

Why do it?

Developing enterprise in your organization means finding profitable ways to sell your skills and expertise to a variety of audiences. To do that, it helps to break those resources down into separate components. Individual staff skills, specific programs, even physical assets such as your building, are all potential earned income generators.

What to do:

1. Call a two hour meeting of the Enterprise Team.

2. Put six large sheets of newsprint on the walls.

3. Write one of the following headings on each sheet.
   - organizational expertise
   - individual staff skills
   - programs
   - print and media pieces
   - physical assets (building, grounds, vehicles, computers, equipment, library, collection, etc.)
   - other

4. Ask the Team to list the organization's tangible and intangible assets in each category. Be as thorough as possible. The more assets on your sheets, the more possibilities you'll have for earned income ventures.

5. Give the Team this example to help them get started:

The rhumba is an asset to music. No, no! That's the wrong one. Try this one:

The Center for Occupational Hazards is a clearinghouse and consulting service on common workplace hazards. A small organization in rented space, they approached this exercise thinking they had few assets. To their surprise, they made the following lists:

organizational expertise:
• in-depth knowledge of workplace hazards, methods of prevention and treatment, and practical and legal issues surrounding them

individual staff skills:
• knowledge of chemistry, labor law, physics, business law, mediation techniques, environmental regulations, political and lobbying experience

programs:
• seminars on workplace safety and workplace regulations
• consulting services on reducing workplace hazards, on working with labor unions
• mediation services between management and labor
• training program for managers

print and media pieces:
• information and training videotapes on workplace safety
• booklets on individual hazards and their prevention
• workbooks on uncovering and eliminating hazards in your business

physical assets:
• office space, 1000 square feet
• classroom, 700 square feet
• two computers with database software
• computerized telephone message machine capable of giving 20 prerecorded three-minute messages

other:
• reputation for comprehensive, high-quality work; for approaching problems responsively and reasonably; for saving clients headaches and money
• ability to confer an unofficial, but valuable, "safety seal of approval" to organizations
• access to lawyers, doctors, researchers, politicians

Making the list helped the Center recognize marketable assets. Possibilities were: renting message space on their phone machine to other organizations; creating an official Safety Seal of Approval: organizations would pay the Center to inspect them in order to earn the Seal; selling booklets on worksite hazards and prevention to insurance companies to use as premiums for their business customers; renting their classroom to other organizations needing meeting or classroom space; selling training seminars on occupational safety to business schools; selling videotapes and training materials to Chambers of Commerce and industry trade groups to distribute within their areas.

Using the Information:

Congratulations! Each of the assets you've listed is a potential earned income generator. Keep reading to find out how.

CHAPTER 11:

Examining Your Markets and Market Trends

"If the person is over 40 years old, I tell him he
should do something because it is first good for
Japan, good for the company, good for his family and
finally good for him. If the person is under 40, I tell
him he should do it because first it is good for him,
good for his family, good for the company and finally
good for Japan."
—Ken Hayashibara,
Japanese manufacturer

FADE IN. The room is a third-floor walk-up on New York City's lower West Side. Truck brakes squeal and car horns bellow below. Through thick cigar smoke we see Herbie shifting from one foot to another, like a man waiting for the restroom . . .

Herbie: L-look, what about Tidy & Teary, they're a great act. Tidy comes on wrapped in the American flag and Teary throws a bucket of white flowers —

Lupe: The Watergate burglar and the psychedelic guru?

Herbie: Right! Perfect for your July 4th weekend, so Americana.

Lupe: C'mon now.

> [Lupe draws another cloud from her stogie, then releases it in Herbie's direction. She places her left boot on her desk.]

Herbie: Okay, okay, how bout Clarissa the penguin impersonator? Such a sweet person, always a favorite, how can you miss with laughs like that?!

Lupe: It's a convention of maitre d's, fer chrisakes!

Herbie: Right, well then, Phillipe, Phillipe the food magician. After he makes his entrance from a bell-shaped chafing dish, he produces then disappears a 20-gallon tub of potato salad — mayonnaise or German-style, your choice — before . . .

> [Lupe turns away, shaking her head.]

Herbie: Special deal, single day price for the whole weekend. The man is magnificent with bagel and lox.

> [Lupe groans.]

Herbie: Wa-wait, hold on. The Chiccolini Chimps, now there's a great —

Lupe: Herbie, Herbie. I run a business here. Tell you what, give me Lee Jeffries, the comic. He's funny, he's the best ya got.

Herbie: I don't handle Lee anymore.

Exercise #1: Subdivide your current market

Why do it?

You need to know your audience. Traditionally, nonprofits think of their audience as one tidy, homogeneous group. They fail to differentiate subgroups with different needs, interests, skills, income levels and behaviors. This shortsightedness limits their effectiveness in serving – and attracting – different markets.

A history museum, for example, serves children and adults; history buffs and "lay" people; parents and grandparents; teachers and school administrators; university students and professors; tourists and locals; collectors and appraisers; ethnic groups and people with disabilities . . . the list goes on and on. The audiences overlap, but each group can be served – and reached – differently.

Segmenting the audiences provides many benefits. It allows an organization to tailor programs to individual groups, enabling them to serve each audience better. It enables them to market more effectively by targeting publicity material to the interests, styles and emotions of different audiences. It enables them to schedule programs when target audiences can come. Segmenting even provides an opportunity to rethink the fees charged for services.

What to do:

1. Call a two hour meeting of the Enterprise Team.

2. Look at your audiences. List all the sub-groups you can find.

3. What are those groups' needs and characteristics? How can you serve them differently to serve them better? Ask yourself "what if's?" What if you changed the times of your programs? What if you changed their locations? What if you offered different programs?

4. Tell the Team the following story. It will help them get started:

   The Canadian National Institute for the Blind had always assumed their clients were low-income. So they charged minimal fees for their service, relying heavily on government funding. After segmenting their audiences they realized they came from multiple income brackets. In fact, a large percentage were middle and upper-middle class. This realization enabled CNIB to increase their fees for selected services, making some services self-supporting.

Exercise #2: List your missed markets

Why do it?

Nonprofits tend to assume the current audience is the only audience. They fail to ask, "Who *else* needs or wants what we can do?" As a result they miss opportunities to serve and prosper.

Freeze your assumptions about who you serve. You've always served poor people in the inner city? That doesn't mean you should serve *only* poor people in the inner city! There may be other groups who want the same products and services. Maybe they can pay higher prices and subsidize service to your original audience. It pays to look and see.

What to do:

1. With the Enterprise Team, study the products and services you currently offer.

2. Ask yourselves, "Who else might need or want what we do?" List as many new audiences as possible.

3. Tell the Team the following story. It will help them get started:

   Swope Parkway Health Center is a walk-in clinic in a low-income neighborhood in Kansas City, Missouri. For years it relied on government funding for support. However, government contracts declined, and as competition from other health providers heated up, Swope found itself needing new sources of income.

   As the staff took stock of the variety of services they offered, they realized their modest-income neighbors were not alone in needing them. Middle and upper income people also need those services, and in fact, are willing to pay for them.

   So Swope opened a satellite mental health center in an office complex. Their strategy was to attract more middle and upper income clients who had private insurance, which pays more for mental health services than the state system.

Exercise #3: List trends that affect your markets

Why do it?

Nonprofits often assume the current audience is the permanent audience. But the world is not stationary. Allegiances change; the fashionable becomes passe. Technology, scientific discoveries, political movements, weather patterns – all creating new groups of people with new needs. The changes may surprise us, but they shouldn't *take us* by surprise. Your current markets' needs will change, but new markets are forming that will need your service.

What to do:

1. With the Enterprise Team, look at the changes that will effect your field in years to come. List as many as you can.

2. List the ways each change will affect your organization.

3. List some ways you can take advantage of each change.

4. Tell the Team the following story. It will help them get started:

The mission of the Vancouver (British Columbia) YWCA is to provide training and support services to women. Their services range from career planning to home economics, from renting inexpensive hotel rooms to running fitness classes. While their charter does not specify a target audience, the majority of their constituents are low-income. However, with government contracts and traditional funding shrinking, the YWCA needed broader markets. When they examined trends affecting women, several things stood out:

1) 60% of all new workers are women, creating a need for job training and career counseling for women at all socio-economic levels.

2) By 2031 one fourth of all Canadians will be over 65. The majority of these will be women, who will need senior support services.

3) As Babyboomers age, so do their parents. Since most caretakers of elderly parents are women, there is a burgeoning need for support services for caregivers.

4) Many Babyboomers are choosing to stay home with their babies. These women seek parent education and activities to do with their children.

5) The high rate of divorce has created large numbers of working single mothers. These women need child care as well as help creating quality time with their children.

Examining these trends, the YWCA identified five *new* markets:

> working women
> older women
> women caring for senior parents
> young mothers at home
> working mothers

Each of these markets can be served by existing in-house expertise.

Among the new programs the YWCA is considering:
> parenting classes
> informational publications
> informational seminars
> videotapes

Income generated by some of these programs will support free and low-cost services for the YWCA's traditional audience, women in need.

Using the Information:

Each group you have listed is a potential new market for your products and services. Keep them in mind as you develop ventures and look for corporate partners.

 Ask, "Who *else* needs or wants what we can do?"

An outlandish spring rite

CHAPTER 12:

Brainstorming Possible Ventures

"A hunch is creativity trying to tell you something."
— Frank Capra,
film director

Exercise: Brainstorm possible ventures

Why do it?

An earned income venture is a product, a service or a special event that you create and sell at a profit. Venture ideas come from matching your skills and expertise with market needs, and brainstorming is your chance to get a ton of ideas on the table. Get your most creative, trusted minds together and let them loose for two hours of unrestricted daydreaming.

The process will invigorate you if you don't hold back. Brainstorming is like a mental "walkabout," the rejuvenation treks of Australian aboriginals. As you mentally walkabout, look for importance in everything; nothing is irrelevant; nothing is foolish. As you share each other's ideas, those ideas gain value, they grow, they mature. One seemingly silly idea leads to a "brainstorm." So be prepared to walkabout.

What to do:

1. Schedule a two-hour meeting, early in the morning (7:30 to 9:30) so people are fresh. Hold the meeting away from the office, away from telephones and interruptions. Tell people they may *not* go to the office first: you want them thinking creatively and long-term, not distracted by today's concerns.

2. Invite two key, free-thinking staff people, one key, free-thinking Board member, and two or three outsiders whom you value for their creative thinking. (Outsiders are vital because they're not bound by the history of the organization.) Have no more than seven people in all. Give everyone background information on the organization: brochures, the questions and answers you've generated so far, and maybe this book.

3. Designate one person as Chief Meeting Organizer and recorder. His or her role is to keep the conversation going, keep it focused, and take copious notes. Your Enterprise Champion is the ideal person for this job. He or she must be a good listener because he will be writing more than talking.

4. Start the meeting with rolls and coffee. Give people a few minutes to wake up and warm up, then list your organization's operating adjectives. Make it as long as you can, then look ahead three years. What adjectives should describe you then?

5. That should get you off and running. If the second list is representative of your operating style, what kinds of programs will you offer? What products might you sell? Who will want to buy them? What businesses will want to work with you?

6. Standard brainstorming rules apply: no one can criticize an idea. All ideas are written down. Quantity is as valuable as quality. The point is to get as many ideas as possible on the table. One idea often leads to another.

7. If you get bogged down, ask: "Who needs what we've got to offer?" And, "We know who's out there; what can we do for them?" Remember, you've frozen your assumptions about how the organization operates. Right now, anything is possible.

8. The process of brainstorming builds slowly, but by the middle of your session you should be shouting, gesticulating and interrupting each other as ideas pop into your heads. Quit at two hours on the dot (before the energy starts to lag). Congratulate each other on your ideas. Then have the list typed up. It's the job of the Enterprise Champion to prioritize the list later. Don't be surprised: you'll have more ideas than you'll be able to use.

Using the information:

See Chapter 18.

> *"Nothing is more dangerous than an idea*
> *when it is the only one you have."*
> —Emile Chartier,
> *philosopher*

CHAPTER 13:

Defining Your Future

*"More and more these days I find myself pondering
how to reconcile my net income with my gross habits."*
—John Kirk Nelson

Exercise: Flesh out your fantasy

Why do it?

In "Evaluating Your Style" (Chapter 9) you defined your organization's future operating style. In "Examining Your Markets" (Chapter 11) you found new audiences for your programs. "Brainstorming Possible Ventures" (Chapter 12) gave you a list of projects you might offer. The picture of your new entrepreneurial organization is taking shape.

Now let's add some weight. There are many other aspects of your organization that you want to control: finances, building, staffing, public image . . . All these will influence your ability to deliver your mission in the most effective way. By defining goals in these areas now you clarify your vision. You start making your fantasy real.

The following exercise asks you to describe how your organization will look and feel to insiders and outsiders, and to overlay that information on the programs, markets and operating characteristics you have already defined. It asks you to create a holistic, concrete vision of your organization three years from now.

Why three years? Three years allows you enough time to engineer significant changes yet it's close enough for everyone to set their sights on. There's an urgency in three years that will keep your momentum going once you start moving toward these goals.

What to do:

1. Hold a two hour meeting of the Enterprise Team.

2. Hire an illustrator to attend the meeting. He or she will hear the "raw" emotional concepts of your organization, and will be able to give shape to them in simple sketches. These renderings will become important communications tools.

3. Imagine it's four years from now. Look back on year three and answer the questions below.

4. As you answer them, think big! Freeze your assumptions about your organization's limitations; let your excitement and imagination carry your goals farther than they might otherwise go. Don't just say you'll break even: say you'll have money in a cash reserve. Don't just say you'll have more visitors than you have now: say you'll double your attendance. Remember that, unlike the traditional nonprofit, entrepreneurial organizations always push their limits and challenge their own expectations. Think creatively now, or you'll never achieve big goals.

5. At the same time, be realistic; you need a future vision that is grounded in reality. Do this by creating a logical extension of who you are now. Push your limits, but give yourself time. Don't promise too much too soon. Your vision should be achievable in incremental steps. You must see the path to getting there and you must be able to make your constituents and investors see it too. Your constituents will need to believe in your organization if they are to ride through your changes with you. They should be your proudest boosters as you grow. Investors are vital because you need them to launch ventures; you can't do it without them.

6. To paint a picture that is big *and* realistic, answer the following questions in the past tense. Talking about what you have already accomplished will keep you pegged to reality.

7. Make your answers quantifiable. Include measurable proof of your accomplishments. Don't just say you had money in a cash reserve, say how much you had in the reserve. Don't say your staff liked working there; give evidence that that was so. Is turnover measurably lower? How much lower? Are salaries measurably higher? How much higher? By quantifying your goals, you can measure your progress toward them.

8. Develop a vision with teeth: bring a new business person into the process. Ask someone who isn't a board member, who will bring all his or her business sense to bear on the situation. Tell him that his job is to play the role of skeptic, or better yet, the role of potential investor. As you go through the questions, his job is to challenge every answer; to push for the kind of answers he'd want if he were considering putting $250,000 into your organization and expected a return. Pick someone caring, but tell him not to be kind. He must be honest, insistent – almost irritating – if he wants to help you.

> *"Where there is no truth, there is no kindness."*
> —Nachman of Bratslav,
> *ardent 18th century cabalist and ascetic*

THIRD YEAR QUESTIONS

Imagine it's four years from now. Look back on year three and answer these questions.

1. You received three fan letters from customers. What did they say?

2. *Fortune* magazine cited a major accomplishment of yours. What did it say?

3. The mayor of your city cited a major accomplishment. What did she say?

4. What did your balance sheet look like?

5. Your calendar was filled with appointments in year three. With whom did you meet?

6. You added five new board members. Who were they?

7. Describe your physical space.

8. One CEO of a major corporation turns to another and says, "Imagine that! That organization actually _____ !" What did he say?

9. A major foundation head gives a speech that begins, "I didn't think it was possible, but (*your organization*) actually did _____ ." What achievement is he extolling?

10. What were your major activities of the year?

11. Who were the customers for each activity, and how many were there? What did you charge them?

12. Draw your staff organization chart.

13. At your year-end profit-sharing party, the staff gave testimonials to what they like about the organization. What did they say?

Using the Information:

By answering these questions, you've put a lot of flesh on the fantasy of your new entrepreneurial organization; you've made it less a fantasy and more a realizable vision.

"SEEMORE the CNIBee"

CHAPTER 14:

The Promise Only You Can Make

*In 1985, a Rochester (NY) supermarket chain
advertised for "part-time career associate
scanning professionals." In other words,
they were hiring checkout clerks.*

Exercise: Make your list of "only's": the things only your organization can do.

Why do it?

Your vision is not only a picture of the things you'll do in the future. It's a positioning statement. It's a definition of the things you do better than anyone else. In your crowded field of endeavor, it's the reason people come to you.

We live in an age of specialization. Doctors are no longer general practitioners; they are internists, cardiologists or other single-system specialists. Sneakers are no longer all-purpose sports shoes; they are running shoes, tennis shoes, basketball shoes, aerobics shoes, each specialized to the demands of an individual sport.

Even department stores, which once dominated merchandising with their offers of something for everyone, are now carved into specialty stores within stores. How else to compete with the plethora of specialty boutiques that offer just one kind of merchandise but in every conceivable shape, color and size? It's no longer credible to offer something for everyone. Consumers demand the depth, quality and quantity that specialization brings.

To succeed, that specialization must be promoted. It must become inherent to the image of the product or business; it must become the reason consumers want to use it. Successful businesses are good at this.

As an example, Scandinavian Airline Systems (SAS) could have marketed itself as "the best airline in Europe." But that would have been a grandiose, unbelievable claim. Instead, it decided to be "the best airline for frequent business travelers in Europe." SAS picked a targeted audience with definable needs, changed its way of doing business to meet those needs, and then marketed its ability to those people.

A less substantive approach might be Proctor and Gamble's. They could have marketed Wisk as "the best all-purpose laundry detergent." But that claim is so broad it becomes bland and unbelievable. Instead, they sell its ability to eliminate "ring around the collar." By targeting a specific, recognizable need, they create credibility and desire for their product. Soiled collars remain and Wisk sells on.

The same opportunities are available to nonprofits. Specialization sells. Quality specialization endures. To attract customers you need to do one or two things and do them well. Whatever your field, you need to single yourself out from your competition by being the best in your area of speciality.

What to do:

1. Hold a two hour meeting of the Enterprise Team.

2. Make sure your professional skeptic is there.

3. Define your area of specialty, the one or two areas in which you will set the standard for your field. Ask yourselves:
   What do you do that no one else does?
   What do you do better than anyone else?
   Why will people come to you instead of to your competition?
   What is the promise only you can make?

4. Tell the Team the following story. It will help them get started:

   Swope Parkway Health Center, the Kansas City comprehensive health clinic in the low-income neighborhood, had falling attendance rates and a reputation for low staff morale and long waiting times. As part of an overall plan to strengthen the organization, they have decided not to be all things to all people, but to serve their immediate neighborhood very well. They have initiated a publicly advertised policy of "Dignity Care" in which they offer the kinds of service people expect from expensive private hospitals: guaranteed minimum waiting times; valet service; and roses for all new mothers. Behind the new policy is Swope's positioning statement: they now define themselves as "the best health clinic for modest-income people."

Using the results:

You will use this information to shape the slogan and visuals that will describe your organization to the public.

See the USA in your

CHEVROLET

Communicating the Vision

"Every picture tells a story, don't it?"
—Rod Stewart,
rock & roll singer

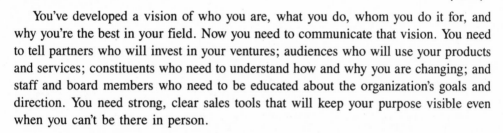

Exercise: Create a slogan and visuals

Why do it?

You've developed a vision of who you are, what you do, whom you do it for, and why you're the best in your field. Now you need to communicate that vision. You need to tell partners who will invest in your ventures; audiences who will use your products and services; constituents who need to understand how and why you are changing; and staff and board members who need to be educated about the organization's goals and direction. You need strong, clear sales tools that will keep your purpose visible even when you can't be there in person.

What to do:

1. Start by writing statements you think reflect your vision. Write them several ways until you come up with one that says it all. (Remember: this isn't a mission statement. Mission statements are like personnel policies: important, but boring. They help the staff but don't inspire the public. You want a statement that tells your public you've got what they want.)

2. When you get a statement you like, take it to a professional copywriter. Explain your vision, your audiences and what you need the statement to achieve. Ask him to put some "sizzle" in your slogan. Take time to look at various copywriters' portfolios to substantiate each person's experience and talent, and do not underestimate the value of professionals who have spent years honing their craft.

3. If you have not already done so (Chapter 13), hire an illustrator to translate your verbal pictures into drawings. Choose your illustrator with the same care that you did your writer. You've been "painting" your vision all along. Now it's time to put it on paper so other people can see it too.

4. Pick up to five venture ideas that typify the "new you" and explain them to the illustrator. Ask him or her to draw the activities in use.

If, for example, you'll be producing educational books for families, have him draw families enjoying the books together. Make sure the titles, subjects and your organization's name are quickly visible.

If you'll be developing exhibits for shopping malls, show people using an exhibit in a mall. Always make sure your name and the subject are visible. It doesn't matter if you don't know the exhibit's content yet. You know enough about your field and the exhibit's goals to make an educated guess. The drawings can be simple black and white renderings. They don't need to be fancy. They do need to be legible and professional.

5. Before you release the artist and copywriter, test your slogan and pictures on three potential users of your products and services. Ask each one:
   Would you use us?
   How much would you pay?
   How will you be different afterward?
Test the pictures and slogan on potential investors and colleagues, too. If they don't get the desired responses, change them until they do.

Using the results:

The Slogan

Adopt the slogan as a tag line to your name. Put it on your stationery and business cards. Add it to your logo. It should tell the public in one crisp sentence what you are about, so use it to promote your mission and message wherever people see your name.

The Visuals

Include them in funding proposals to teach corporations and foundations about your organization. Include them in your newsletter to tell members where you are going. Use them in promotional materials that describe your goals. Include them in press packets. Use them to recruit board members. Blow them up to 16″ x 20″, mount them on foamcore and use them in-house to show to staff, board and visitors.

Together, your slogan and pictures will be your principal sales tool for communicating your vision to the public and investors. Boldly and quickly they should say: this is who we are. We're focused in our vision. We're entrepreneurial in our outlook. We're not like any other nonprofit you know.

FROM STATEMENTS TO SLOGANS

Organization	Their Vision Statement	Their Final Slogan
Institute for Nonprofit Organization Management, a nonprofit management consulting firm	We are the national resource for informed nonprofit decision-makers who are striving for organizational effectiveness.	We specialize in nonprofit turnarounds.
AddVenture Network, a non-profit marketing consulting firm	We develop marketing strategies, products and services that diversify nonprofits' income.	We change the way nonprofits do business.
Swim, B.C., a recreational and competitive swim center	To generate revenue and resources to support the goals and objectives of selected sport and recreation agencies through worldwide leadership in the development of aquatic products, services and education.	We are your competitive edge.

Easy Way to better pict

CHAPTER 16:

Updating Your Fantasy

Mussolini had a clear, inflexible vision of himself which not even Heaven could alter. On arriving there, he found only one mirror which everyone had to share. The waiting line was endless. Undaunted, Mussolini strode to the front and pushed aside Napoleon who was buttoning his tunic.

"I am the Duce," intoned Mussolini.

"I am Caesar," called a voice from behind. "Yet I have the patience to wait."

"Not I!" said Mussolini.

Those in line began to grumble and a major altercation seemed imminent. Suddenly Machiavelli approached.

"Peace, friends," Machiavelli urged, then whispered something into Mussolini's ear. Whereupon Mussolini swaggered from the mirror and took his position at a distant tree. There, he folded his arms, and stuck out his chin and chest.

"What," asked Churchill in amazement, "did you say to him?

"I told him," said Machiavelli, "that in a few minutes the line would form over there for the photographer."

* * *

Don't get stuck on your organization's image. You need to continually update it. Think of it as a Polaroid photograph that takes three years to fully develop.

As you take advantage of new opportunities, your vision should be flexible enough to accommodate them. Nonprofits tend to want permanence — to establish a path and stick to it forever. Alas, the world is in flux and you have to continually respond to its changing demands. So review and update your vision regularly. Every four- to-six months measure your performance against it. Are you delivering on your promise? Is the promise still accurate? Make adjustments. Then snap a new photo.

USE YOUR ENTERPRISE TEAM TO ...

1. evaluate the results of your organizational questionnaire
2. develop your lists of current and future operating characteristics
3. list your tangible and intangible assets
4. divide your current audience into its many sub-groups
5. examine who else needs or wants the things your organization can do
6. examine trends that may affect your markets and how you can capitalize on them
7. brainstorm earned income ventures
8. define where you want your organization to be in three years
9. define your organization's area of specialty
10. review the slogan and visuals that will communicate your vision to the public.

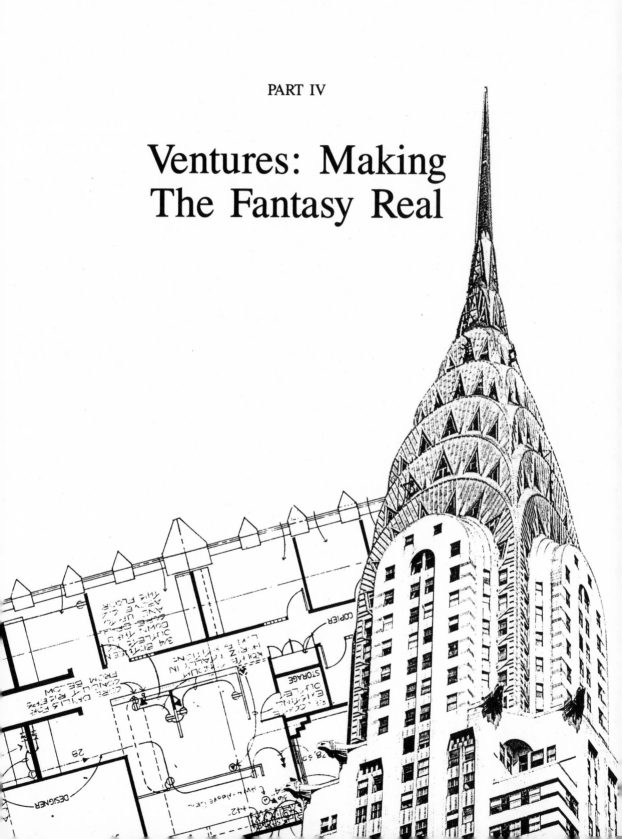

PART IV

Ventures: Making
The Fantasy Real

CHAPTER 17:

What Is A Venture?

Thomas Edison often remarked that the standard for
his inventions was the silver dollar. "If it don't come
up to that standard," said the great inventor, "then I
know it's no good."

Section III of this book talked about developing an entrepreneurial vision for your organization. This section talks about turning that vision into profit-making ventures.

Ventures are projects that fulfill your mission and make money. They are distinct from "programs" which serve your mission, but do not necessarily make money. Some of your existing programs may be "repackagable" as money-makers; others may continue to serve a valuable purpose in their current form. Hopefully, your new profit-making ventures will subsidize programs that don't pay for themselves. Your organization's catalog of activities will probably always include both types of projects.

CATEGORICALLY SPEAKING

Typically, ventures fall into three categories: products, services and special events.

Products

Products are books, kits, videos, calendars, clothing, equipment . . . any tangible item you produce. However, unlike typical nonprofit products which are sold retail to individuals, profit-making products are wholesaled to corporations for use as premium items. They can also be used as membership or fundraising incentives within your organization.

THE SMOKING POLICY INSTITUTE

The Smoking Policy Institute develops smoking-control policies for businesses. While that sounds simple on the surface, it is actually a complex process that involves legal, financial, labor union, morale, enforcement and education issues.

To guide companies, the Institute provides customized consulting and instructional workbooks and videotapes. Retailing these to the end user is costly and time-consuming. Instead, the Institute has wholesaled its products and services to Blue Shield health insurance.

Blue Shield distributes the products and services to *its* clients in several ways. The products are premium items they use to attract large business customers. They are perks they offer to preferred customers. They position Blue Shield as concerned with customers' health. And because smokers use more health care than non-smokers, encouraging companies to limit workplace smoking enables them to offer all their customers lower insurance rates.

For the Smoking Policy Institute, the joint venture produces guaranteed cash on bulk sales, and introduces them to many companies they would never reach on their own.

Services

Most nonprofits are in the service business, yet few turn services into earned income ventures. Doing that is not difficult: position your service as something that can be sold to corporations for use by their employees and customers. That's what the Smoking Policy Institute did with their consulting services, above.

Teaching, counseling, nursing — almost any service can work this way. Package an existing service for bulk corporate sale, or develop new ones. Be creative in thinking about what you have to offer. What skills exist in your organization that can become a service for corporate employees or customers? Here are some examples:

SAMPLE FILE

A SPORTS MEDICINE CLINIC

A nonprofit sports medicine clinic in the Midwest has been researching, diagnosing and treating sports-related injuries for ten years. Patients come through referrals, advertising and word of mouth. While business was good, it was unpredictable. The clinic had no way of knowing how many patients it would see each month, and how much income it would receive. The clinic wanted to expand its patient pool and stabilize its income.

To do this, it sold a package of services to the city school district. It now provides prevention education services to each junior and senior high school, and receives a monthly retainer to serve students who become injured during school sports. The contract not only stabilizes the clinic's income, it gives them access to an important audience. Their sports injury prevention message is being heard by a lot more people.

SAMPLE FILE

VANCOUVER FAMILY SERVICES

Vancouver Family Services does counseling for low- and middle-income people. Their clients come on a drop-in basis or through referrals from social service agencies. Most pay little or nothing. As a result, Family Services was looking for ways to produce greater, more predictable income, and to reach new populations.

They have contracted with several local corporations to provide counseling services to employees. The corporations hire Vancouver Family Services on an annual retainer. The fee, based on the number of employees, covers a specified number of employee visits per year. If more employees seek the service, the corporation is billed for additional visits.

Special Events

Special events put your organization in the public eye and reinforce your image and message. Even more important: they make guaranteed income before they take place (unlike traditional nonprofit promotional events, which provide goodwill and anxiety for the staff).

Special events are developed on a theme that relates to your mission and includes ways for corporations to participate. Whether through display booths, consultations, films, or seminars, businesses should be able to purchase time and/or space to communicate with your audience. Of course, their participation must be high-quality and of value to your audience. Ordinary product ads and displays should be discouraged in favor of ones that teach important information. You want your audience to learn and enjoy – not to endure a sales pitch.

Help your business partners develop quality presentations and build that time into their fee. It's one more way you'll help them stand apart from their competition. Price each form of participation relative to its level of exposure. Sell as many of each form as you need to cover all costs of producing the event plus a profit. Charge an entry fee at the door, and keep those gate fees as profit.

Special events benefit from repetition. Whenever possible, make them annuals. Repetition strengthens the event's reputation; it builds expectation in the public; and it enables you to capitalize on all you've learned in previous years. Staff, volunteers and partners recreate the event with greater efficiency and profits improve.

Watch for signs of aging, however. Even the most popular events get tired, so keep them fresh by deleting and adding aspects. Then quit on a high. Four years is as long as most events sustain excitement with the public. Don't wait for yours to slide. Launch a new one. That will save you overestimating income projections when the event starts to sag, and will foster your image as a dynamic organization, always ready with something new. Allow nine months to a year to get a new event off the ground.

Time your special events to correspond with lows in your budget cycle. Special events provide chunks of cash, so use them to fill cash flow holes. But never do more than four events a year. Large events have a tendency to be disruptive no matter how well organized they are. One event per quarter is tolerable. More than that invites cries of mutiny.

What kinds of events can you do, and who could your sponsors be? Here is an example:

SAMPLE FILE

COLORADO ACADEMY

Colorado Academy is a private school in Englewood, Colorado. They wanted to help parents find constructive summer activities for children, and also wanted to generate income before the summer financial doldrums.

So the Academy held a Summer Opportunities Fair. Summer camps, dude ranches, tour outfitters, sports facilities, and other summer activity providers bought booths and paid to place ads in the Fair program book. It provided an excellent opportunity to reach their target audience.

But the school didn't stop there. They wanted the event to be free to families, so they developed three additional income sources. They sold a corporate partnership to Domino's Pizza: for a large fee Domino's was listed in the program and had a booth at the Fair. The Academy rented food and drink concession stands and took a percentage of the sales. And they sold their mailing lists to the businesses that bought booths so those companies could have further contact with Fair attendees. Fees paid by the business participants exceeded the costs of running the Fair and Colorado Academy netted $10,000.

THEMES NATURAL TO US

Sometimes ventures group themselves naturally into themes. As you brainstorm possibilities, you may find products, services and special events that serve the same audience, or that relate to the same subject. Take advantage of it. Group those ventures into a package and give the package a name. Make it a major thrust of your enterprise strategy.

THEMES ADVANTAGEOUS

There are several advantages in creating a package of ventures:

1) **Ventures can reinforce each other.** Having multiple ventures that appeal to the same audience or relate to the same theme enables you to say, "If you liked our videotapes, you'll love our classes!" For-profits call this cross-promotion.

2) **Venture packages help define your organization to the public.** If you can explain what you do in two or three large themes, your mission – and your vision – will be easily grasped.

3) **Defining packages may lead to new ventures.** Singling out an area of need or defining an area of activity may uncover additional products and services you can offer.

SAMPLE FILE

VANCOUVER YWCA

As mentioned in Chapter 11, the Vancouver YWCA examined trends and found five expanded markets: working women, older women, women caring for older parents, women at home with young children, and single mothers. As they examined the needs of each market, and the programs they could offer in response, the YWCA found the needs and programs grouped into three areas: information and support; career development and leadership training; and increased service to their traditional audience, women in need.

Setting the year 2000 as their goal for full program development, they created three packages, or initiatives:

Information 2000

In a world of rapid change, Information 2000 positions the YWCA as the principal source of information for women. It is an umbrella term for publications, tapes and classes which offer information on subjects from child care to fashion.

Women 2000

Women 2000 is a leadership development program. Under its umbrella the YWCA will spawn networks between women in leadership roles and programs to help women cultivate leadership skills.

Service 2000

Service 2000 is a promise to deliver high-quality programs to low-income women. Under its umbrella, the YWCA will create a self-perpetuating endowment fund to support those programs.

The three initiatives support the YWCA's belief: "We help women cope and excel."

SAMPLE FILE

THE WESTERN INSTITUTE FOR THE DEAF

The Western Institute for the Deaf has a double mission. They provide counseling, interpretation and job placement services to the hearing impaired; also handicap prevention and education services to the general public. As Western Institute examined venture possibilities, they realized that all of their ideas focused on one of two goals: to popularize handicaps by removing stereotypes about the disabled; and to prevent handicaps by educating people about unsafe behaviors. So they naturally created two initiatives: Popularization and Prevention.

Popularization

Under the umbrella of Popularization, they are creating a variety of products and services that teach the public about handicaps. A portable mall boutique sells handicapped dolls and children books, and a traveling exhibit uses participatory activities to teach about disabilities.

Prevention

Under the umbrella of Prevention, WID markets products and services designed to help prevent hearing impairments. These include Hearing Stimulation Kits for infants, "Sound Smart" kits to help people recognize unhealthy practices such as overly loud stereos and worksites; and windshield screens with a "healthy ears" message.

CHAPTER 18:

Choosing A Venture

June 10, 1975
The day the U.S. Army gave a whole new meaning to having a birthday blast. Picture this:

The New York Yankees are celebrating "Army Day" at Shea Stadium (where the team is playing while Yankee Stadium is being renovated). Two 75 mm cannons stand in centerfield, facing the American flag. (Army brass have assured the team that the cannons' paraffin will flash harmlessly.)

You're ready for this, right?

As the crowd waits in anticipation, a battery from Fort Hamilton fires the first salute. An ear-splitting boom shakes the stadium, followed by one, two, three more blasts. Smoke fills the stadium. The crowd shimmies with earthquake vibrations. What's this? Glass shatters in the lofty Diamond Club.

Uh-oh. They've blown out more than candles. They've taken out three panels of centerfield fence and a fourth is on fire. This party's over.

Even Walter Cronkite can't resist commenting: "Army 21, Fence 0."[3]

You may want to start enterprise with a bang, but you also want to leave your fences standing. How do you begin? With which venture should you start?

LOOKING AND LEAPING

The most important thing is to have a plan. Make sure you have a clear idea of your overall goals, and of how your venture will contribute. It should serve your mission, reinforce your public image, and relate to other ventures you will do.

Be equally clear about the venture's goals. Is its purpose to reach a certain audience? To convey a certain message? To make a lot of money? Most likely, it's all three. Is that achievable? Be realistic. Too often nonprofits take on ventures because they *want* to do them, only to find afterwards that they didn't meet their goals. Don't be surprised.

Occasionally you may decide to do a venture that doesn't make a lot of money. That's okay, but choose that consciously. Realize the opportunity cost of doing it. Make sure the other reasons justify the time. Make sure your next one brings in big bucks.

STRAIGHT AND NARROW

To choose a venture, narrow your list of possibilities to the three with the greatest potential. These are the ones that are simplest to do; that go straight to your strengths; that require skills you have in-house; that fit your mission and vision; and that require the least capital.

When you've got three top choices, test them a little further. You need to know if the assumed market really exists, how much it will pay, and how much it will cost to produce the venture. It's time for a common sense feasibility study. Grab your paper and pencil, and test your top three ideas against the following nine questions.

NINE CRITERIA FOR SELECTING A VENTURE

1. Relativity. You don't have to be Einstein to calculate if the venture is related to your mission. It should be to go forward! Of all the criteria, this is the most important. It is important to your Board, to your constituency, and most important, to those bureaucratic demons at the IRS or Revenue Canada. As long as your earned income ventures are mission-related, your income will not be taxable. If you're unsure of whether something is related, consult a tax attorney who is familiar with nonprofit enterprise. You *can* choose to do an unrelated venture, but that's not the easiest first step.

2. Profitability. To determine a venture's profitability you will need to do a *pro forma*. This is your "best guess" estimate of your venture's income and expenses. The pro forma doesn't have to be lengthy or complex. A few phone calls to people who are familiar with that type of project should give you most of the information you need.

Direct costs. First, look at your direct costs in producing the venture. Include labor, materials, transportation, equipment rental, special services, postage, photocopying, and any other expenses that may be incurred.

Indirect costs. Next, look at your indirect costs. These include administrative staff time, secretarial time, rent, utilities, insurance, telephone, and any other costs that will accrue to your organization to support the development and operation of this venture.

Markets. Look at your markets. Who will want to buy this venture? How much will they buy? How much will they pay? Once you have these basic figures on paper, juggle them. Look for as many ways as possible to lower your costs and raise your revenue.

Variables in producing a venture. There are many. For instance, who makes the product or delivers the service? Who distributes it? Who advertises it? What if you had the book printed in Hong Kong? What if you hired a fulfillment house to distribute it rather than hiring a staff person? What if you hired contract staff to deliver the service rather than using staff on payroll? Can your corporate partner advertise your product or service so you don't need to pay for advertising?

Variables in selling a venture. Can you sell the same premium item to two businesses in different fields? Can you sell the item as a premium and also retail? Can you pre-sell a publication to corporations and also to a publisher?

What if's. If the venture seems profitable, do some market "what ifs?" What if paper costs rise and expenses increase 25%? What if half as many businesses buy the book? What if they'll only pay half the price? Develop best and worst case scenarios. In its worst case, will the venture still turn a profit?

Expert second opinions. Have your industry experts look over your figures and challenge your assumptions. Ask them to be conservative: most ventures fail because their planners underestimate expenses and overestimate sales.

Know your financial goals. How much money do you want this venture to make? Don't just make a profit; make enough of a profit to justify your time and effort.

3. Cash Flow. The cash for producing a venture should come from your corporate partners, not from you. However, some ventures take cash upfront for mock-ups (samples) or to do research. Will this venture drain cash when you can't afford it? Will it produce cash when you need it? Pick a venture that matches your ability to finance it.

4. Image. Every venture should deliberately build your public image. Will its character, audience, quality and message project your organization the way you want to be seen?

SAMPLE FILE

BRANIFF AIRLINES

In 1987, Braniff Airlines ran an ad campaign targeted to Hispanic communities. On Spanish-language television and radio stations, Braniff attempted to woo customers by offering leather seats. The radio commercials told listeners to fly Braniff "*en cuero*," which means "in leather." But a similar Spanish expression, "*en cueros*," means "naked" – and the two phrases sound identical when spoken quickly.

As we all know, TV often has more impact, and sure enough, the TV version was an eye-opener, inviting travelers to fly *"en cuero"* and *"con tres pulgadas mas,"* meaning "with three inches more." Presumably the airline was referring to extra leg room, but those viewers who thought the voice-over said *"en cueros"* received an entirely different message.[4]

5. Know-how. Do you know enough about this type of venture and this subject to do it well? (If you're going to speak to the Hispanic community, do you speak Spanish?) Are you comfortable with the venture's level of complexity? Who on your staff can manage it? Is knowledgeable, affordable outside help available?

6. Opportunity Costs. Every decision to do a venture includes a choice *not* to do a different one. What revenue will you not make because you didn't do the other? Will this venture provide enough benefits to compensate? Have you maximized profitability on all other projects before starting a new one? Aim to do fewer ventures with bigger payoffs, rather than many projects with smaller returns.

7. Resources. Does this project make the best use of your staff, time, expertise, money, program strengths, image and physical assets? Are the resources you'll put into it proportional to the outcome? Proportional to your organization's size?

8. Love. Do you love it? Do you really want to do it? Will your staff and board get behind it and support it? Your passion for the venture will be your greatest sales tool. Love means never having to say you're sorry.

9. Demand. You may have a great idea for a venture, but if you can't sell it, it's not worth much. How many businesses or individuals will want to buy it? How much will they buy? How much will they pay?

To answer these questions you need to measure the market. The research doesn't have to be extensive – or expensive. There are simple ways to gather the information. And of course, we're going to show you how. Turn the page.

CHAPTER 19:

Market Research

NOSEY PARKER'S FOOTSTEPS

During the early years of the first Queen Elizabeth's reign, Archbishop Matthew Parker of Canterbury found himself between church reformers and dogmatists in the bitter fight over church doctrine. To Parker the question was, "What do the People want and need?" So step-by-step he investigated specific issues rather than the larger rhetorical ones. (Not surprisingly, the origin of the word "investigate" comes from the Latin "follow a footprint.") Though risky, Parker's investigations led him to renounce Puritanism, to moderate church defections, to write the first privately printed English book, and to eventually earn him the label "Nosey Parker," a term that lives on today, more than 400 years later.

It's time for you to pick up the scent. In doing market research, follow one footprint at a time. Do not ask questions beyond your reach. Start with manageable ones.

Then, will people buy your venture? You'll never know for sure until you actually do it. Enterprise is for people who are willing to take risks! But a little market research can take some of the anxiety out of the process, and can give you useful data for plugging into your pro forma.

"Don't use research like a drunk uses a lamp post;
use it for illumination, not support."
—David Ogilvy,
advertising kingpin

FUNDAMENTAL QUESTIONS

The point of market research is to answer some fundamental questions: Is there an adequate market for the venture? How much will people pay? What's the competition? Will enough people buy yours to make the venture worth doing? Do the people understand what you are selling? Contrary to common belief, you don't need to hire a research firm, hold focus groups, talk to people in shopping malls, conduct telephone interviews or spend a lot of money to find the answers. You do need to talk to people who *have* done those things.

And you can be sure someone has, no matter how arcane the data may seem. From the American Pencil Collectors Society and the National Pygmy Goat Association to the Flying Funeral Directors of America and the Desert Fishes Council, some group somewhere has collected the data you need. Your job is to find out who. Fortunately, your first step is small and easy to take. In just eight places you'll find most of the information you'll need.

EIGHT EASY PLACES

1. Industry trade groups and the Yellow Pages

As with the pro forma, your most important source of information will be people who do this type of venture all the time. They not only know costs and procedures, they know their markets. They will assist you with pricing, sales trends, consumer attitudes, competition, and other information that helps you gauge the market for your venture. Industry trade groups produce publications and compile research that is generally available for free. Use them and the Yellow Pages to find experts in that field. People love talking about what they do; they will generally give you as much information as you want.

2. Popular magazines

If you want information on your target markets, read the magazines they read. Look at the issues that are discussed. Look at the products and services that are advertised. Ask the magazine to send you their readers' profiles. These will give you information about their ages, incomes, lifestyles and buying habits. Run your idea past people in the advertising and editorial departments; they sell to their readers all the time, they know what they buy.

3. Research groups, national social service agencies, government agencies

If you are contemplating a venture that addresses a particular social need, consult an agency in that field. They will help you define the need, the market and probable solutions. The local government and public library can help you find the right agency.

4. Chambers of Commerce

If you are planning to sell a venture to a local business, consult the Chamber of Commerce. They know the local business scene.

5. Brokerage houses

If you are considering a venture in a particular industry, or thinking of selling a venture to a company in that industry, go to a brokerage house that analyzes that field. They can give you industry costs, profits and trends, and information on the companies you're considering approaching.

6. The public library

The business section of your public library is a gold mine of information on individual companies and industries. You can find a particular company's advertising budget, staff size, vice presidents' names, and other information that will help you evaluate their buying potential (plus, help you make sales contacts later). Particularly helpful are:

The Standard Directory of Advertisers
Also known as the Advertiser's Red Book, it lists companies doing national or regional advertising.
Standard and Poor's Register of Corporations, Directors and Executives
Lists corporations and their officers, Standard Industrial Classification codes, annual sales, number of employees, subsidiaries, and more.
Dun and Bradstreet's Billion Dollar Directory
Provides detailed marketing data about the top U.S. parent companies.
The Insiders Guide to Small Business Resources
Lists a wide range of information sources, from entrepreneurial advisors to sources of funds.

Make friends with the business librarian and have him show you the ones most useful to your venture.

7. Business magazines and newspapers

Reading business magazines and newspapers is vital for several reasons. They will help you stay on top of trends in the market; they'll give you ideas for new opportunities; they'll reinforce your market-orientation and enterprise attitudes. The business section of your local newspaper is equally important. Look for trends in the local community; businesses that are doing well and might be ripe for a venture, and stories about new or unusual executives who might be open to working with you.

8. Lovers, friends and potential users

When you've exhausted these resources, and you've winnowed your list of possible ventures to the two or three that seem most likely to succeed, do some informal data gathering among people whose opinions you respect. Start with people closest to you, the ones who want to keep you from humiliating yourself. Then move out to people who have known you for a long time and know your capabilities. Finally, talk to people who might actually buy your venture. Ask each person, Would you buy it? How much would you pay for it? How would you be better after using it? Ask people who you know will give you honest answers; they'll be your most valuable market research tool of all. Trust them.

Another word about market research. It won't buy you certainty. Nothing does. (Ironically, Matthew "Nosey" Parker was also chaplain to Anne Boleyn, whose passions led to too much research. She didn't know when to stop sampling.) Enterprise is for people who know when to stop juggling numbers and take a risk. Trust your gut; don't go beyond and lose your head.

 Keep research expense in proportion to your investment and expected return.

 No amount of research will guarantee success.

CHAPTER 20:

Pricing

You've heard the first rule of real estate, "location, location, location"? Well, the first rule of sales is "price, price, price." It's great to develop and sell a product or service, but if you can't price it to make a profit, you might as well not do it.

Pricing is a poker game, a bluffing match. Every venture, every person has a price above or below which he won't go. We call that the Walk Away Price or, in poker parlance, the "Cattle" Hand.

TEX LAGGARD

Tex Laggard was a cattlehand in the Old West. Like the other grizzled men of the sage and cactus, he was ready as he'd ever be for the roundup. All the men were. 'Cept they had to share the cookin' while they were out on the range, and not a man in the group could cook a lick. It was hard being out there in the heat and dust. But what was hardest was the food. It was gawdawful. Still, no one dared complain; first man to say somethin' nasty bout anyone else's cookin' — he had to cook for a week.

By the third week out Tex Laggard was gettin' ornery, he was starvin' for some decent food. As much as he hated to cook himself, he sure loved to eat. But he had a bad feelin' about what dinner'd be like tonight. Pug St. Claire was cookin' and Pug was the worst cook of the bunch.

When Tex sat down next to the other boys, not a one of 'em was eatin'. Everybody was starved just ten minutes before. They all just sat there lookin' at each other, the stew steamin' up out of their bowls, everyone sniffin' and kinda turnin' away, not sure.

Tex looked over at Pug St. Claire and the old buzzard had his back to the group and Tex couldn't tell if Pug was coughing or sneezing or what. But damn! Tex was hungry.

"Well come on boys, ya gotta eat . . . " said Tex picking up his big old soup spoon, " . . . Ya know the rules." He dove into it. All the men lurched forward. Even St. Claire glanced over his shoulder in surprise. There was a moment, nothing more, before Tex' eyes turned to pinpoints; then the disbelief . . .

"This tastes like cow patties!"

Every man gasped; St. Claire glowered.

Then Tex remembered how he hated to cook, "Tasty though."

* * *

Tex Laggard had his Walk Away Price, his "Cattle" Hand; no way was he going to cook for a week. That was his bottom line. You need to hold a Cattle Hand, too, everytime you sidle up to the poker table of business partnerships.

YOUR CATTLE HAND

In your case, as an enterprising nonprofit, it's your costs. That's where you draw the line. You're going to need accurate accounting of both direct and indirect costs.

Direct costs are the labor, materials, printing, transportation, photocopying and other "hard" expenses incurred by the venture.

Indirect costs are the portion of your overhead that you can attribute to the venture: salaries, rent, utilities, insurance, etc. You can compute your indirect expenses based on actual time spent and space used, or you can apply a percentage of your budget. If you use a percentage, be sure it's high enough to adequately cover the costs.

Total your direct and indirect expenses and never sell a project for less! Never! In fact, don't sell a project for that price either, because you'll forfeit your profit. Add some profit to your costs and make that your Walk Away Price. Tex Laggard and Pug St. Claire both had bottom lines. Your Walk Away Price has got to be yours.

BLUFFING FOR FUN & PROFIT

The easiest *and* safest way to price something is with "cost plus" pricing. That means you start with your costs and add on a profit to reach your sales price. Start by doubling your costs. That's called "keystoning." The 100% keystoning markup covers your competence, credibility and expertise. Many businesses price merchandise at "keystone plus 25%" or more, so don't be afraid of overpricing.

Typically nonprofits underprice. They fear if they price something too high, the corporation will permanently reject the deal. They won't! If a company is interested in a venture, they'll always listen to a lower offer. If you've started negotiating too low, however, you can never get the price back up. Remember: designer genes!

DON'T LOOK NOW, BUT IT'S THE BIG BOYS

Nonprofits are so used to small numbers they forget the scope of a corporate budget. They forget that businesses are used to paying large amounts for services and that they value what they pay for. Make sure your price to a company is one they will take seriously.

For example, a small nonprofit that specializes in dispute resolution sold a package of services to a large corporation. Midway through the contract, the company's Personnel Manager, the man who had hired the organization, approached the nonprofit's director. "You know," he said, "you guys are doing great work. You've eliminated a lot of tension in our company, and I have to say, I'm surprised. I didn't think you'd be able to do it. I mean, I knew you'd do something good – but I didn't think it would be that good. Your fee was so low, I just didn't think we'd get that much for it."

With a corporate budget of close to a billion dollars, the Personnel Manager was used to spending hundreds of thousands of dollars a year on services for his employees. In his way of thinking, $16,000 (the fee charged by the nonprofit) couldn't buy enough time to produce a quality product.

WHINE COUNTRY

Your price should have enough of a sting for the company to feel your confidence and professionalism. They should say "ouch" before accepting it. They may whine about the price, but that's OK. It increases the value of the venture.

As an example, several months ago Richard did a seminar in Spokane, Washington. His normal fee for a day-long seminar is $75 per person, but because this seminar had been underwritten by a bank, the per person fee had been dropped to $25. One hundred eleven people had pre-paid and registered for the session, but when he got to the hotel, a quarter of them hadn't come.

Richard was surprised. Generally his seminars play to full houses. "Oh, don't feel bad," his host assured him. "It's been raining here a lot and today is a beautiful day."

What she didn't add was that at $25 people could "afford" to skip his seminar. At $75 they wouldn't have considered it. Not enough "ouch" in that price!

NEGOTIATING

Unfortunately, pricing is not always a matter of stating your price and then shaking on the deal. Frequently you have to negotiate. That's why, before you go into any sales meeting, you do your homework. There are some things to know to negotiate effectively.

1. Know what the market will bear. Talk to people in the advertising business and the business you plan to approach. Find out what corporations generally spend on this type of activity. Are there companies that provide similar services? What do they charge?

2. Know your variables. There's more than one way to produce your product or service. What can you add or subtract to change the price? If a four-color book is too expensive, sell them three-colors. If your proposed oddball page size overshoots their budget, switch to a standard size. If small-group employee seminars strain their budget, offer one class for the whole team. The better you know your product and its options, the better deal you'll cut.

3. Know what the corporation has to spend. You probably won't find out exactly, but by doing some snooping you can get a good idea. Nosey Parker lives! If it's a national company, look in *The Standard Directory of Advertisers* for the company's advertising budget and breakdown. That will tell you how much they allot for this type of venture annually. Get as much information from your contact as you can. Press gently but firmly.

4. Hold off establishing a price until after your first sales meeting, if possible. Once you've got the corporation interested, they will be more open to negotiating price, and during your meetings you can extract information that will help you price the venture accurately. Here's an example of how this happens.

THROWING THE LAMB CHOP PAST THE WOLF

Jennifer Sawyer is Director of Enterprise at a senior center. The organization has an idea for a booklet called "In Celebration Of Aging," a compendium of stories about men and women enjoying their later years. She is pitching the idea to the Vice President of Marketing at a retail drug store chain.

> **V.P.:** Okay, what's it going to cost?
> **Sawyer:** Well, first let's talk "what if's." How are you going to use this book? Do you want a self-liquidating premium or a free one? Do you want people to pay a little bit for it, or do you want to give it away free?
> **V.P.:** I think we have to go free on this one. We've tried self-liquidators in the past and they haven't worked so well. In fact one time —

Sawyer: — Alright, how many copies do you think you'll need? Give me a range — minimum, maximum.

V.P.: Uh, well, we're opening a new store in a couple of months in an area that's heavily populated with retirees. If we offer it as an opening give-away — our gift to the community — we could probably use 10,000. Ya, 10,000 would probably do it. Could we get more if we ran out?

Sawyer: We would own the copyright. You could buy more. But your second printing costs would drop. Of course, if you bought more the first time around, your per unit costs would drop considerably.

V.P.: I suppose we could buy more, but I'm not sure what we'd do with them. I don't want to get stuck with closetsful.

Sawyer: Could you use them as a sales-inducer in one of your other stores — give one away with every purchase over $10.00?

V.P.: Maybe. Actually, we could give them to our major suppliers too. If we did that, we'd probably need 100,000.

Sawyer: Whoa! That really changes your price. On numbers like that you will see your per unit costs drop.

V.P.: That's true . . . Well, tell you what, give me a price on 10,000, 50,000 and 100,000. I'll have to go over this with our CEO, and that way we'll have enough information to make a decision.

Sawyer: How much do you generally spend on a premium like this?

V.P.: It depends. Sometimes the company buys them. Sometimes it's up to individual stores. When the company buys them we can spend more. Say up to 50 cents apiece. The individual stores won't spend that much. They usually won't go past 25 cents.

Sawyer: 50 cents will buy you a slick, four-color piece, if the larger quantities hold. For 25 cents you're probably looking at something two-color, a little smaller. Fewer pages.

V.P.: I'm not promising anything, but we'll look at it both ways.

Sawyer: Your new store opens in March, so you'd want the booklets delivered by February 15?

V.P.: Yes, that'd be great.

Sawyer: Fine. I think I've got it. I'm going to get you prices on 10,000, 50,000 and 100,000 in two price ranges: under 25 cents and under 50 cents. Right?

V.P.: That should work.

Sawyer: Fine, I think we have made a good start. I'll get back to you in a few days with prices.

Through this exchange, Sawyer whet the vice president's appetite without letting him take a bite out of her meaty sales pitch. What's more, Sawyer gleaned a lot of information that will help her price the booklet in a range the company can afford. She's also picked up useful information on the company that will help her with later ventures. If there's one criticism, it's that Sawyer cut off the V.P. when he was about to reveal past problems with self-liquidators. Valuable information was lost because Ms. Sawyer wasn't listening. Overall, though, a good meeting.

Nonprofits tend to accept the first deal that's offered. They aren't used to wheeling and dealing. Often the first offer is not the best. If you've established a price for your venture that you know is competitive, don't give it away for much less. Tell the corporation you think you can do better. Go talk to their competitors. If the corporation thought there was any merit in your venture, that alone may bring them back. If not, you may find a better deal next door. At any rate, never offer a product or service without a reasonable profit margin for your organization. It's not good business.

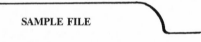

SAMPLE FILE

THE DAIRY BARN

The Dairy Barn is a small arts center in Athens, Ohio. In 1980 it came up with an unusual — and lucrative — idea for a special event that would give the center wide national recognition. The event was the National Jigsaw Puzzle Championships, a lively two-day contest in which jigsaw puzzlers from across the country would compete in the art and sport of puzzling.

The Dairy Barn sold the concept to Hallmark, makers of Springbok puzzles. For Hallmark the event was a natural. It gave them a chance to unveil their new line of puzzles. It gave them a chance to associate with a high quality institution, and it gave them tremendous national publicity. Over 700 puzzlers gathered to compete for the title of "world's fastest puzzler." Others submitted entries for new puzzle designs. The event was covered on Good Morning America, in Sports Illustrated and in other media Hallmark could never have afforded to purchase. Clearly this was an event to repeat.

They did. The two partners went on to do the National Jigsaw Puzzle Championships for four years in a row. The fifth year, however, Hallmark changed the rules. Because of internal changes in the company, Hallmark management wanted to rewrite the Championships contract in a way that was less favorable to the Dairy Barn. Shrewdly, the Barn refused. They knew they had a hot item, and they decided to take it elsewhere. Their savvy paid off. They offered the Championships to American Publishing Company which bought it on the Dairy Barn's terms. The two new partners went on to do the event for another two lucrative years.

"Keystone" to price your products and services. Double your costs
to create your profit.

Example:

				Keystone		
(25 cents)	+	(25 cents)	+	(50 cents)	=	($1.00)
direct expenses		indirect expenses		profit		sales price

CHAPTER 21:

Finding Corporate Partners

"Familiarity, truly cultivated, can breed love."
—Dr. Joyce Brothers,
psychologist

Finding the right partner is not a chance affair. Patience, homework and common sense will point you to companies likely to buy your venture. Be your own match-maker: look for companies whose markets, image and interests companion your own. The closer they match, the more likely a partnership.

DO THE SAME PEOPLE INTEREST YOU?

Match point #1: Look at the audience. **Any corporation that wants to reach the people you serve is a possible partner.** Look at the buying habits of your markets. What do they buy? Who do they buy from? Those businesses can use your help to reach their customers.

SAMPLE FILE

SWIM, B.C.

Swim, B.C. is the provincial swimming association in British Columbia. Its goal is to interest people in the sport of swimming, and train competitive swimmers. Al Heather, Swim B.C.'s Executive Director, read the book, "Mentally Tough," which suggests that corporations use sports training techniques to hone their corporate competitive edge. Instantly he recognized a potential venture. He called Peter McLaughlin, the book's author, and proposed a joint seminar for corporate executives.

Using techniques developed by Swim, B.C., author McLaughlin would train executives in the principles of his book. The seminars, which would be held at Swim, B.C., would be expensive and exclusive, and everybody would benefit. Executives would learn valuable techniques, McLaughlin would publicize his book, and Swim, B.C. would gain visibility and recognition. In the process they would also meet corporate executives (all of whom would be potential venture partners) and they would make money. McLaughlin agreed.

The next challenge was to find a corporate partner. If the seminar was to make money, it needed to be organized as a special event. All costs would need to be covered up front. Money from seminar attendees would then be profit. What company would want to partner such an event? The answer was another question: what company wants to reach leading corporate executives in the United States and Canada? Well, there are many possibilities. Banks, brokerage firms, equipment manufacturers, and telephone companies, to name a few.

Al Heather approached several corporations, and after a few phone calls and meetings, Kodak Copier Division agreed to partner the seminar. Together, Kodak, Swim B.C. and McLaughlin developed the "Mentally Tough Seminar." Held in the spring of 1988, it attracted 270 attendees and netted $10,000 for Swim B.C. The organization also strengthened its visibility and image, and favorably impressed 270 corporate executives with its ability to conceive and manage a business venture. Kodak, for its investment, reached that many potential business customers with a product and message they valued highly. Because of the success of the seminar, the three partners are now planning how to take the event national in 1989.

INTRODUCTIONS BY RELATIVES

Match point #2: Look at field of endeavor. **Any company in a business related to yours is a possible partner.** What companies make products or provide services that relate to your field or to the subject of your venture? Associating with you will increase their credibility with their customers.

SAMPLE FILE

DAIRY BARN and SHOPSMITH

Remember the Dairy Barn, the small arts center in rural Ohio? They developed a second partnership with Shopsmith, manufacturer of power tools. When the Barn wanted to produce a traveling show on the art of woodworking, they needed underwriting for the costs. Enter Shopsmith. The show was perfect for their marketing needs. It associated their tools with the finest woodworking in the nation, and placed their name squarely before their target audience. In fact, Shopsmith not only underwrote the show, they advertised it. They enclosed entry forms in all their orders, putting word of the show in the hands of 40,000 woodworkers.

NOT-SO-BASHFUL ADMIRERS

Match point #3: Look for demonstrated interest. **A company that has already demonstrated an interest in your organization's area of specialization** is an obvious prospect. If they are already interested, you won't have to work hard to convince them. Working with you – an expert in the field – will better help them achieve their goals.

SAMPLE FILE

SMOKING POLICY INSTITUTE, redux

When the Smoking Policy Institute wanted to build business, they designed a seminar for corporate personnel managers. The seminar would introduce managers to the problems of smoke in the workplace, and (parenthetically) suggest that the Institute could solve them. But how to reach the managers? Easy. They went to Prudential Life Insurance Company. Prudential had long encouraged business customers to implement health promotion programs. That positioned them as caring, and lowered employee claims. Taking that reasoning one step further, the Institute suggested that Prudential sponsor its smoking seminars around the country and invite its business customers to attend. Prudential agreed. They liked the opportunity to strengthen their caring message; the Institute got its message heard for free.

FAMILIAR LINES

Match point #4: Look for compatible marketing themes. **A company whose marketing theme is similar to yours, or similar to the theme of your venture**, will be interested in what you have to offer. Your venture will give concrete form to the abstract values they espouse in their campaign, and will reinforce their campaign in the mind of the public.

SAMPLE FILE

UNITED BANK OF DENVER

When United Bank of Denver launched its "We Challenge Ourselves For You" advertising campaign, the Denver Children's Museum saw an opening for a venture. Challenge and children go hand in hand in the Museum's way of thinking. Many of the Museum's exhibits and products encourage children to challenge themselves to learn and grow. So the Museum approached the bank with an idea called the Children's Challenge Award.

The Award would be a statewide contest to honor children aged seven to eleven who had challenged themselves and excelled in art, science, community service, courage, or other areas. The bank would advertise the contest in statement stuffers, ads and signs, and would receive nominations.

A committee of bank and Museum staff would screen all the nominations. Finalists were then turned over to a Blue Ribbon panel of local celebrities for selection of the winners. Winners would receive a plaque, lunch, and $500. United Bank loved the idea. It made real their campaign theme of excellence and self-challenge. It demonstrated their commitment to their state and customers. The bank paid the Museum $22,000 to organize the event, half of which was profit to the Museum.

SAMPLE FILE

THE GIRAFFE PROJECT

The Giraffe Project is a national nonprofit that encourages people to "stick their necks out" to make a difference in society. Giraffe directors recognized a natural partner when they saw an ad in the newspaper for a large insurance company. The company's campaign slogan was "Everyone can make a difference." What a perfect match for the Giraffes!

They quickly put together a package of ventures that would meet both parties' needs. The two organizations are currently negotiating the series of ventures. We'll tell you more about them in Chapter 22. They will provide benefits to the company's employees. They will reinforce the company's slogan. They will spread the Giraffe's message and earn income for the Project.

LOOKING FOR MR. DO GOOD

Okay, so you're ready to get familiar with potential partners. How do you find companies that match your interests and audiences? By using the same techniques and resources you used for market research.

1. Make a habit of reading business publications. They will help you understand how businesses think and what they're looking for. *The Wall Street Journal, Ad Age, Report On Business, Fortune* and *Inc.* are fun to read as well as informative.

2. Look for feature stories about unusual companies and executives. Those that are singled out for interesting reasons may be more open-minded, more savvy, and better prospects for unusual ventures.

3. Look for advertising slogans that put a premium on values. Words like "excellence," "leadership" and "achievement" which mesh with your own intangibles, can give you a hook to hang a venture on.

4. Call the marketing department. When you find an ad that suggests its company is a likely partner, call their marketing department. Find the person who approved the ad. Tell him why you liked his ad (people love compliments) and why your organization is a good match with his. Don't call the ad agency. Agencies have a way of forgetting or distorting ideas that aren't their own. What's more, they have no bottom line reason for passing your ideas onto their client.

5. Look at companies that are acknowledged for their values. *100 Best-Companies to Work for in America and Canada* and *America's Corporate-Conscience* are books that list companies that take pride in the same values you do. They may be likely partners.

6. Check existing research on corporations. You can find information about companies you're interested in by studying existing research generated by United Ways, Chambers of Commerce, banks, brokerage houses, industry associations and magazines. Often they'll let you use it for free.

7. Go to a company that holds second position in its field whenever possible. They need to work hard to catch up; they may be more willing to try the unusual.

FINAL PREPARATIONS

Once you've reduced the field of possible partners to two or three, do a little more homework. Gather as much information about those companies as possible. Consult the *Standard Directory of Advertisers* and other trade publications. Read the corporation's annual report. Find out their advertising budgets and the breakdowns of how those budgets are spent. That will give you an idea of how much money they might have to spend on your venture. Get the names of their CEO and marketing executives so you know whom to contact.

Look at their past advertising campaigns and products. Does your venture jive with things they've done before? Talk to people who know the companies, gather as much information as you can. All this data will help you structure ventures to best meet the companies' needs.

The more you read, the more you talk to people, the more in touch you are with the business world, the easier it will be to spot potential partners and get familiar with them. Like everything else in enterprise, it's a matter of attitude. Once you start thinking like a business person, you'll start attracting them.

Of course, business partnerships are like any other; they're based on mutual satisfaction. As soon as one partner is unhappy, the relationship generally ends. So keep in touch with your partners' needs and keep them mindful of yours.

CHECKLIST:
Corporate Venture Guidelines

As you design your ventures, you will find it helpful to think about them from your potential partner's point of view. Keep asking yourself: Will this meet several of the company's needs? Will it be

---

easy to implement? Will it work for their audience?

Payless Cashways, the national home building supply chain, expects the following qualities in a joint venture with a nonprofit. Keep them in mind as you develop your own ventures. They will give you a good idea of what your potential corporate partners will be looking for.

COMPANY: Payless Cashways

GUIDELINES FOR: A joint marketing venture with a nonprofit

1. The theme of the venture should:
   - be "warm and fuzzy" and appeal to customers' altruism
   - be simple, distinctive and easy to grasp
   - appeal to as wide an audience as possible
   - promote our marketing message
   - strengthen our image as good public citizens
   - be related to our line of business, if possible

2. The venture should promote sales and/or build traffic to our business.

3. The venture should appeal to employees. It should offer them a way to be involved and, if possible, control elements of it.

4. The venture should be easy to operate. It should be managed by the nonprofit (or an outside contractor) and should require little time from corporate staff.

5. If the venture starts locally, it should have regional and/or national roll-out potential.

6. The venture should be easy to explain and defend to shareholders.

7. The venture should be newsworthy and appealing to the media.

8. The venture should be compatible with our corporate giving guidelines.

9. The venture should be low risk.

10. The venture could have a seasonal focus.

11. We should have exclusive rights to the program.

12. The venture should encourage the nonprofit's members and users to participate.

13. The structure of the venture should allow for corporate review at predetermined checkpoints.

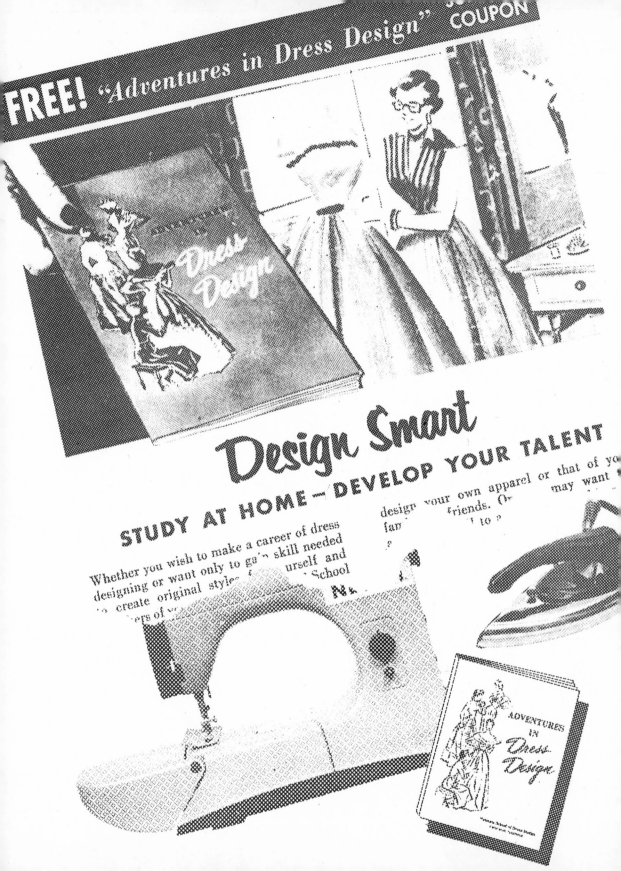

Design Smart

STUDY AT HOME — DEVELOP YOUR TALENT

Whether you wish to make a career of dress designing or want only to gain skill needed to create original styles for yourself and members of your family... School

design your own apparel or that of your family... friends. O... may want to...

ADVENTURES IN Dress Design

CHAPTER 22:

Structuring Ventures for Sale

Three Legs Up

Found on the grounds of a Japanese amusement park:
musical bath slippers; a fig tree that dances to the
music of Karen Carpenter; and a display of
underwear with three leg holes. The garment is
supposed to last for six days, with the wearer rotating
it 120 degrees each day — and then wearing it inside
out for three days.
— Wall Street Journal, Oct. 16, 1987

We all love choice, even if those choices sometimes seem a tad unbelievable. Giant sunglass shades for automobiles and Oreo-crumble ice cream turned out to be legitimate favorites, right? So it's not surprising that on the way to market, the successful entrepreneur offers his partners choice too, to insure their support.

When advertising executives sell corporate clients on a new campaign, they don't present just one option. They go in with a number of ideas because they know their clients like to choose. Selling a venture is no different.

Choosing makes people feel smart and in control. So when you propose ventures to a potential partner, don't offer just one option, offer three. But no more. They'll enjoy picking the one that's right for them, and you'll increase your chances of success. At least one of your three options is likely to be on target for meeting their needs, interests and budget.

TERMS OF ENDEARMENT

Your three options should include ventures at different price points, so they can pick the price that fits their budget; and ventures with a range of complexity, so they can choose their level of time, effort and involvement. Make some options "turnkey," that is, requiring no effort on the part of the company. Make others more interactive, giving company employees, distributors, suppliers or even customers, a chance to be involved. If possible, offer ventures that meet both internal and external needs: something that benefits the corporation's employees, as well as something that boosts its image with customers.

You will also strengthen your proposal if you can offer the company a mini-

131

marketing campaign rather than a list of isolated options. That means offering a logical series of ventures that take place in succession. Each one reinforces the others and reminds the public about the corporation's partnership with you. By building an ongoing relationship this way, you become an integral part of their marketing strategy. The longer the campaign lasts, the stronger your relationship will be, the more interest the corporation will have in insuring its success, and the more likely they'll want to repeat it.

SAMPLE FILE

GIRAFFE PROJECT, redux

Remember the proposed project between the Giraffe Project and the insurance company? It is actually a series of ventures that form an ongoing campaign tied to the company's marketing theme. With the following package of options, the Giraffes meet their own goals of encouraging giraffe-like behavior, and help the company substantiate its slogan, "Everyone can make a difference."

1. *The National Giraffe Award*. Annually the insurance company would recognize a small number of people who had stuck their necks out and made a difference in their communities . The Award would be administered by the Giraffe Project, for a fee.

2. *Giraffes: The Book*. The joint publication of a book chronicling inspiring stories of "giraffes." The book would be tangible proof of the company's commitment to its theme, and would provide a profit to the Giraffe Project.

3. *The giraffe insurance premium check-off*. To reinforce its commitment to making a difference, the company would give $1 to the Giraffe Project each time a subscriber checked this box on his premium.

4. *The Giraffe Contest*. In this special event organized through schools, children would be invited to write stories about courage and community service. Winners would receive scholarships from the company. The Giraffe Project would receive a fee for administering the contest.

5. *Corporate Giraffe Award.* Annually, the company would recognize a small number of corporations for promoting giraffe-like behavior among employees and in their communities. The Award would position the company as the exemplar of courage and community service. They would pay the Giraffe Project a fee for managing the project.

To promote well-being among company employees, the Giraffe Project also proposed:

1. *Internal Giraffe Award.* Annually the company would recognize employee-nominated internal "giraffes."

2. *Giraffe Project memberships.* For corporate employees and customers, purchased wholesale from the Project for use as a premium item.

3. *A Giraffe Service Package.* For employees that includes employee seminars on developing giraffe-like behavior; a children's growth chart that enables families to measure moral as well as physical growth; and a kit of family activities that encourage giraffe-like behavior.

OPPORTUNITY KNOCKS AND KNOCKS AND KNOCKS...

Another thing to keep in mind when structuring a venture is to maximize its income opportunities. Sell each venture many ways to many partners, and try to build multiple income streams into each one.

SAMPLE FILE

THE DALLAS CHILDREN'S THEATER

The Dallas Children's Theater produces an annual Family Arts Calendar. The calendar provides six separate sources of income:

1. The group charges $3,000 for a full page ad. 9 months x $3,000 generates $27,000 a year.

2. For $250 a performing arts group can have its performances listed on the performance dates.

3. For $500 a group can include a discount coupon on the calendar's coupon page.

4. If a patron goes to any five performing arts performances during the year and sends in the ticket stubs, the Dallas Children's Theater sends him or her a free ticket to one of its own performances. Since most people go to the theater with someone, the free ticket usually generates additional paid ticket sales.

5. The calendar is sold in local stores for $6.50.

6. The calendar is also pre-sold at bulk discount to PTA's which sell it at full price and keep the difference. This strategy "mass baptizes" a huge sales force for the calendar, increasing its circulation and winning friends for the Theater.

SAMPLE FILE

THE SMOKING POLICY INSTITUTE, #3

In Chapter 17 we mentioned that the Smoking Policy Institute sells videotapes and workbooks to Blue Shield as a premium item for business customers. But that is just one way the Institute makes money from those materials. They have developed four additional income streams as well.

1. *Pre-sales*. The materials were initially developed in an arrangement with Simon and Schuster. BBP, a division of Simon and Schuster, gave the Institute an advance to create the tapes and books, and published them. Their sales force sells the materials to hospitals and businesses. The Institute receives a royalty on every sale.

2. *Wholesales to nonprofits*. The Institute wholesales the materials to nonprofit organizations in smoking-related fields. The Canadian Cancer Society, for example, buys the materials at discount, then resells them to its own clients.

3. *Wholesales to for-profits*. The Institute wholesales the materials to for- profit companies in smoking-related fields. These companies, which include a smoking cessation company and a manufacturer of hospital equipment, re-sell them to their clients.

4. *Retail*: The Institute retails the materials from its office, through brochures and customer contacts.

Through all of these arrangements, the SPI makes many more sales than it could ever make on its own.

CHAPTER 23:

No-Risk Sales

*New Jersey is not all belching smokestacks and mobsters, but that
is the caricature that often follows the state around. Perhaps that's
why the civic-minded New Jersey Division of Gaming Enforcement
decided to take a no-risk approach to their work. In 1980, the
DGE released its official report concerning local organized crime.*

*The words "mob," "syndicate," "Mafia," and "Cosa Nostra" were
completely avoided, instead replaced with "member of a career
offender cartel." No risk, no pain.*

IF IT'S YOURS, HOLD ON TO IT

We're talking money! And as we've said before: don't use your money, use theirs.
Almost all nonprofit ventures can be done with corporate money. Don't plan the event,
don't write the book, don't build the exhibit, don't spend a dime (except on putting
together your proposal) until you have sold it to a corporation. That way there's no
cash outlay, no unsold inventory blocking hallways, and no risk to you.

Feel like the New Jersey DGE? Sound too good to be true? It's not. Corporations
will use your product or service as a premium item. That means they'll distribute it
(free or for a charge) to their customers or employees. They purchase premium items
all the time. Why not from you?

YOUR THING IS THEIR THING

Here's how it works. You pre-sell the product or service to the corporation. That
means before the product is made or the service performed you sell them a bulk
number of units at a wholesale price. The price includes all your direct and indirect
costs of producing The Thing, plus a profit. Because you have pre-sold it, you are able
to customize it for the corporation. If it's a book, you put their name on the cover or
invite them to put a message from the president inside. If it's a service, you tailor it to
their needs and you hold it at their sites. Once the deal is made, you produce the
product or service at no risk or cost to you.

Imagine you're a literacy organization. You have an idea for a publication – a
parent's guide to helping kids with homework. Who would want such a book? Any
business that wants to reach families with a "we care about education" message. That's

a long list: private day care chains, bookstores, school systems, children's clothing manufacturers, or any retailer or manufacturer selling primarily to families. How to sell it?

THEIR THING CAN BE SOMEONE ELSE'S THING

Pre-sell exclusive rights to a single corporation. In doing research you find that a major bookstore chain is launching a literacy campaign. Perfect! You offer them exclusive rights to your publication. They advance purchase 100,000 copies at a price that covers all your direct and indirect costs plus a profit. You produce the book, put their name on it and agree not to sell the book to any other partner, in any industry, anywhere in the world, at any time. This is frequently the best way to pre-sell something because you can charge a premium price for exclusivity.

Pre-sell to corporations exclusive rights within their industry. Instead of selling the book to just one sponsor, you opt for multiple sales. You know a private preschool chain is opening new centers in your city and needs an enrollment incentive. A local department store is planning a large back-to-school promotion and would like a sales incentive. A local hospital is promoting its improved pediatric unit and could use a take-home reminder of its new services. You offer each of them exclusive use of the book within their field. They pay you to produce the book; they purchase advance copies. In exchange you promise not to sell it to any other preschools, department stores or hospitals.

Pre-sell to corporations priority use within their industry. Two toy manufacturers are promoting new lines of educational toys. You think each would be interested in using the book as a premium. You offer one company use of the book for a limited period of time. They pay you to produce it and purchase copies in advance. For the specified time, they have exclusive rights to the book within their field. (You're free to sell it to a company in another industry.) When the time period expires, you pre-sell the book to the second toy company.

Pre-sell to nonprofit organizations. The local school district is a natural for your book. Pre-sell to the district or the PTA. If they have trouble with the price, get a local bank or retailer to subsidize the purchase. They'll get two nonprofits for the price of one!

Sell to a commercial distributor. You can't find a corporation or nonprofit willing to buy your book, so you go to a publishing house. They agree to publish it. Great for your ego, but bad for your bottom line. Because they take all the risk, you get a tiny percentage of the profits. Make this a last resort.

Use the product or service yourself. Regardless of what arrangements you make with corporations, negotiate your own use of the product. Use it as a membership premium (Join at the $50 level and get . . . "); as a membership inducement (Join now and get . . . "); as a recruiting tool (Sign up a friend and get . . . "); or as a renewal incentive. Always try to use a product or service multiple ways.

PRE-SELLING DO'S AND DON'TS

• DO INCREASE THE PRICE — When you offer a corporation exclusivity, increase the price of the product or service to make up for "lost" sales to other businesses.

• DO PRE-SELL AS MANY UNITS AS POSSIBLE — If you are selling a product, pre-sell as many units as possible because the more produced, the lower the cost per unit. That increases your profit margin (or permits you to pass on a lower cost to each buyer).

• DO NOT BECOME THE DISTRIBUTOR — We will say it again, do not become the distributor of your product. Have it shipped from the manufacturer to the corporation (or to their designated fulfillment house) or you are likely to lose the profit you just negotiated!

   Money — don't use yours, use theirs.

CHAPTER 24:

The Sales Call

My shoes have never done this kind of thing before,
They would not go out in the rain;
It was not me who tracked that mud across the floor,
I don't know how I can explain;
For years my shoes have been my friends,
I've taken them around the world and to its ends,
Now they're taking me . . .
My shoes are
On top of the world,
My shoes are.
— The Bobs,
My Shoes[5]

GIVING YOUR SHOES DIRECTION

You've got three great ideas, all reasonably priced, and a company you know will
love them. How do you get your shoes in the corporate door? Once you're in, how do
you get the company to pay attention? Don't let this sales stuff throw you. Corporate
execs wear shoes just like you; you're already part of the club.

There are a variety of routes into a corporation, and whichever one you pick, your
path to the right person may be circuitous. What you're proposing is new. The
corporation has probably never done this kind of marketing before so it will be hard
for them to know where to begin. It may take three or four phone calls, or even
meetings, to get to the right party. Don't worry, your shoes are patient soles. Plus, it
won't hurt for other players to hear the idea along the way. If your venture goes, it may
involve them, too. Each contact strengthens your image as an imaginative,
entrepreneurial nonprofit.

CALL SOMEONE WHO WEARS SHOES

If possible, start with a contact in the company. If you know the CEO, then by all
means start there! If you've received donations, ask the contributions officer to direct
you. If you've got a product or service for employees call the Vice President for
Employee Relations. If you're approaching the company completely "cold," start with

the Marketing Department. Someone in there must wear shoes. Even within Marketing you have options. Pumps, Oxfords? Who are the high heels? Should you call the Vice President for Marketing? For Advertising? For Public Relations? Public Affairs? Each of these people presides over a different aspect of the company's marketing pursuits — and they all wear shoes! The people in Marketing and Advertising usually have more clout than those in Public Relations and Public (or Community) Affairs, but the latter may be the most initially receptive. Everyone has some affinity for shoes, so don't worry about getting tongue tied; you belong.

BEFORE YOU GET THE BOOT

Wherever you start, the first thing you'll need to do is make clear that you're not asking for a contribution. Corporate managers are used to talking to nonprofits about handouts, not about business deals. It may take them a while to understand that you're proposing a joint venture that will meet *their* needs. Even when they get it, they may be leery of you because nonprofits are often unsophisticated in their approach to marketing, and bear an image of being anti-business. You'll need to defeat those expectations. Remind them constantly that you mean business. Talk in their language. Avoid the jargon of your field.

When you get the Marketing V.P. on the phone, tell him or her that you have a business proposition that will make her money. Be specific, tell her you'd like 15 minutes next Tuesday to talk about it. Know that you are offering the V.P. your organization's valuable name, image and experience. Know that your shoes support you every step of the way.

NO LOAFERS ALLOWED

Once your shoes are through the door, challenge yourself to be even more businesslike than the people you're meeting. Tell them that you know they're busy, that they don't have much time. Remind them you said you'd take just 15 minutes, and put your watch on the table to stress that. You tell them when the time is up. That puts you in control and impresses them with your ability to deliver.

Remember, as you talk, that these people are not philanthropists. They are not there to meet your needs, but rather, to make money for their company. They're entering the meeting with five questions in mind, and you need to satisfy them on each before they will buy your venture. They want to know:

1. **What's new about this idea?** "New" marketing ideas are a dime a dozen. What's new about this one? Why should we get excited?
2. **So what?** It might be a good idea, but why should we want it? How will it benefit us?
3. **Who cares?** Why will the public pay attention? Who will want it?
4. **Doesn't so and so do that?** Didn't our competition already do something similar?
5. **Who are you?** It's a great idea. We can see it will benefit us. But why should we trust you to pull it off?

You want to answer those five questions before they're even asked. Here's an example of how that might work.

All Ears is a hypothetical organization that provides counseling, education and therapy for the hearing impaired. It has recently expanded its mission to include education for the general public to prevent unnecessary hearing impairments. With that goal in mind, Bill Schmidt, the organization's director, called the Vice President for Marketing at the largest local employer. Bill wants him to sponsor Ears' mobile audiology clinic at his plant and in a local mall. The V.P. liked the idea over the phone, arranged a meeting and asked the company's Vice President for Employee Relations to sit in.

Schmidt: Tell me if I'm right: you want to demonstrate to this community that ABC Box Corporation is a genuinely caring and generous public citizen. And you want to demonstrate to your employees that you're concerned about their welfare.

V.P./Marketing: Well, of course.

Schmidt: I've got three products that will help you do it. They're all affordable, competitively priced, and would be exclusively yours. The first one is a turnkey operation. We'd like to bring our mobile audiology clinic to your plant to provide free hearing exams for ABC employees and their families. And we'd like to take it to Southgate Mall for four days during their back-to-school sale to do the same thing. Your name will be on the van. Interested?

V.P.: Tell me more.

Schmidt: First let me tell you a little bit about our organization. Then I'll describe the clinic and how it will meet your needs. All Ears is one of the most respected hearing health organizations in the country. You may already be aware that we've been serving the hearing impaired of Smith County for 9 years, and we just won the Audiology Association Award for excellence in our field.

V.P.: Mmm.

Schmidt: We serve approximately 26,000 people a year with a wide range of services, including hearing screenings, therapy, equipment prescriptions, counseling for the hearing impaired and their families, and education for the general public to prevent unnecessary hearing loss. We are a sophisticated organization with a staff of 6 and an annual budget of $160,000.

V.P./Employee

Relations: What does all this have to do with us?

Schmidt: We've recently begun selling a variety of products and services to diversify our income. The mobile clinic is one of our new services. It's housed in a self-contained 15-foot trailer that will park in your parking lot. It's staffed with three professional audiologists who can handle up to 50 people an hour. They'll do routine hearing tests as well as mini counseling sessions for people who have questions or concerns about their hearing. If the van operates from 8 a.m. to 8 p.m. Thursday through Sunday, we can screen approximately 2,400 people, or all of your workforce plus family members. We can also schedule longer appointments for people who would like them. The normal fee for this service is $10, but your employees would get it for free, courtesy of ABC Box.

(The intercom BUZZES. Frank, the V.P.'s secretary
wants to know if V.P. can take a call.)

V.P.: Tell him I'll call him back.

(V.P. looks back to Schmidt.)

Schmidt: We'll also take the clinic to Southgate Mall for four days in late August. The clinic will park at the main entrance to the mall. A large banner will say "All Ears Mobile Audiology Clinic brought to you by ABC Box Corporation." Newspaper ads and signs throughout the mall will advertise the clinic's presence and that it's available through your company's generosity. Approximately 14,000 people visit Southgate during the last weekend in August. It's their second busiest time after Christmas, and after talking to mall managers they estimate the clinic's presence can increase attendance by 15%.

V.P./Employee

Relations: Is that it? That's an interesting proposal. You know, I have a mother-in-law who's hard of hearing . . .

Schmidt: Well, she may have a lot of questions about what's happening to her if her hearing is suffering. I'm sure she would appreciate the chance to talk to a professional audiologist — for free. And she would appreciate the accessibility of a mobile clinic. She won't have to make an appointment. She won't have to worry about how to get there. The clinic will be open on a drop-in basis, twelve hours a day, in a place where she's probably already going. That's what's so new and exciting about this idea. For the first time, we're taking hearing tests and education to the public, instead of waiting for them to come to us. Did you know that most hearing impairments are preventable or correctable with proper treatment and education. But most people don't get treatment or education because its not usually this accessible. With this mobile clinic, ABC Box Corporation can reach 17,000 people in eight days with information that can prevent hearing loss. You can have a major impact on the hearing health of our community.

V.P./Marketing: 17,000 people in eight days . . . that's an impressive number for a personal contact.

Schmidt: It also reinforces your corporate message that you are concerned about the health and education of your employees and your community. The clinic really makes tangible the promise you make in your ads when you say, "We care."

V.P./Human Relations: You're right about that. But, don't the schools do this? Seems to me my kids get their ears tested every year in school.

Schmidt: Young children get their ears tested in school, but when was the last time you had your ears tested? Schools do a fine job with children up through second grade. After that, most people don't have their ears checked again until there's a problem. Then it's too late. Even when people do have their ears checked — whether it's in school or at the doctor's — they usually receive little education about preventing hearing loss. That's a large part of what the mobile clinic does. We tell people how to develop healthy hearing habits at home and at work. We'll send everyone home with a Hearing Habit Handbook — with ABC Box Corporation's name on it — to remind them how to keep their ears healthy for the rest of their lives. That's 17,000 in-home reminders about how ABC Corporation really cares about their health.

V.P./Employee Relations: Hmm.

Schmidt: Well?

V.P./Marketing: I'm not sold. I think deafness is gloomy. I don't think people want to have their hearing checked. It's not sexy.

Schmidt: *Health* is sexy, one. And, two, people love learning about themselves. Have you ever seen anyone pass up a chance to learn something about himself? Most people can't pass up a bathroom scale, even when they know they won't like what it says!

V.P./Employee Relations: Ha! You've got a point there. But let me ask you a question. We've got a plant down in Springfield. Can we take it down there?

Schmidt: No problem.

V.P./Marketing: And can we do the mall there, too?

Schmidt: You bet.

(Schmidt knows the V.P.s are hooked, but V.P./Employee Relations has paused.)

V.P.: One last question.

Schmidt: Yes?

V.P.: Where'd you get those shoes?

Schmidt's got them hooked, all right. There's a moment in a successful sales meeting when the corporate contact starts saying "we." At that moment he's bought into the venture. That doesn't mean your work is over. There are usually further sales to be made: to his boss, his boss's boss, maybe even to a marketing committee. However, from that point on, your contact will be your ally in selling to the rest of the company. Checking their feet, you're bound to notice . . . they all wear shoes. Members of your club!

TOEING THE MARK

Up until that point, you purposely haven't talked price. Always get them excited about the idea first — make them want it — then tell them what it will cost. Price negotiations should wait for a subsequent meeting. If they like your idea, they'll invite you back. At that time you can gather the information you need to price the venture accurately.

Sales is the creation of a mutually satisfying relationship. Each party wants something the other party has, and the sales meeting is the dance in which you arrange the exchange. Most of its steps are predictable: you know what they'll ask and you can rehearse the answers. Every once in a while something unpredictable happens. They offer the one response for which you weren't prepared. We call it "window of weirdness." It's bound to happen. You can't avoid it. Still, it helps to anticipate that it might happen. So don't be devastated by it.

BABY'S GOT A BRAND NEW PAIR OF SHOES

It also helps to remind yourself that you are your venture's best salesperson. Think about it. Who talked the babysitter into letting you stay up late? Who talked your parents into giving you the car keys when they didn't want to? You did — because you believed in what you were selling, and it showed. The same is true for your venture. No one will believe in it more strongly or communicate it with more enthusiasm than you will. In fact, your enthusiasm, because it's infectious, is your greatest sales tool.

To a corporation your best selling points are that your joint venture is affordable, competitively priced and exclusively theirs.

 If you can't explain your concept quickly and with enthusiasm, forget it.

Get them excited about your idea first, then tell them what it will cost.

CHECKLIST
TERMINOLOGY

It's important in sales meetings to talk the corporate language. That should remind your corporate contacts that you think like they do — in business terms. Start substituting these for-profit terms for their nonprofit equivalents.

For-profit term	*Nonprofit equivalent*
invest	support
investment	donation
investor	donor, funder
partner	sponsor
profit	surplus (or excess funds)
return on investment	well, it was good publicity!

Also, note these internationally different terms.

United Kingdom term	*United States and Canadian equivalent*
charities	nonprofit organizations
companies	corporations
sponsorship	marketing dollars

SAMPLE FILE

TREES, INCORPORATED

Trees, Incorporated is a hypothetical environmental group. They have developed a portable exhibit on their area's ecology which they would like to rent to a shopping mall. Their director, Janet Casey, has secured a meeting with the director of the mall's merchant association, a guy named John Tara. Here's their conversation.

Casey: I've made some assumptions about you. If they're correct, let's talk. If not, we're wasting each other's time. Assumption #1: you need to increase traffic in your mall. Assumption #2: you need to increase your merchants' sales volume and their profits. Assumption #3: you want to show the community you're involved with their concerns. Assumption #4: you need to show your merchants that when you spend their marketing money you get a demonstrable return. Am I right?

Tara: True. You say Trees, Inc. is a nonprofit organization?

Casey: Yes, why?

Tara: You don't sound like a nonprofit type; I mean ... well, never mind, go ahead finish your pitch.

Casey: Okay. Okay I've got something for you that is affordable, competitively priced and exclusively yours.

(Casey pauses)

Casey: You look skeptical.

Tara: (smiling) Maybe a little.

Casey: I have a portable exhibit on our state's ecology. It can be at your mall Thursday through Sunday. It's a turnkey operation: we'll set it up, take it down and staff it. Your staff will have no responsibilities. We'll advertise its visit to your mall in our newsletter which is read by over 5,000 people. According to surveys by City Magazine this area has 50,000 people who consider themselves "environmentalists." 72% of them earn over $25,000 a year. We have a lot of credibility with these people, and many of them will visit the exhibit if you advertise it. Now only will they shop in your stores, they'll consider your center a friend of the cause. The exhibit will cost you $1500 for the four days. I think you and your merchants will find that investment produces a measurable return. What do you say?

At this point Casey has shown Tara that she knows the mall director's business. She's substantiated that he can attract desirable new customers. She's shown he can influence his community image. And she's shown him how he can make himself look good to his merchants. All for only $1,500 which they both know is consistent with the mall's promotions budget.

How does Janet Casey know that? She knows because she's done her homework. She called three other malls and asked how they run promotions and how much they pay. She talked to three merchants about what they like in a promotion, and she talked to the Petting Zoo people who were at this mall last weekend to confirm what she'd learned.

From her own records she has already gleaned statistics on the environmentalist population in the area. That's Trees' target market and the main asset they can sell to a corporate partner. What about their newsletter? Trees has only 2,200 members, but its membership survey indicated that each issue of the newsletter is read by an average of 2.3 people. All this homework put Casey in a strong negotiating position in that sales meeting.

Undercover Strategy

CHAPTER 25:

The Proposal

SAN JOSE, CA. It took firefighters 20 minutes, using wire cutters and needle-nosed pliers, to free a woman from a pair of tight-fitting designer jeans. The woman had borrowed the pants from a cousin.

— The New York Times

Know what you're getting into, and make it equally clear to your potential partner — by putting your proposal in writing. Your first corporate contact probably won't be your last; he will probably have to show it to his boss. Since you can't be at that meeting, you want a "stand in" there, something that will present your venture in its most favorable light. That is your proposal.

THE FOUR-PAGE FITTING

The proposal is a short (four-page!) reminder of what you told your company contact in person. The first two pages are a narrative. They describe the venture in concrete terms and cover the five basic questions of sales (Chapter 24). The last two pages are pictures. They show the venture in action. If the venture is an event, they show people at it. If it's a product or service, they show people using it. People buy things they can visualize, so the proposal makes them visualize success.

The pictures can be simple, black and white line drawings, or quick magic marker sketches. They don't need to be fancy, but they must be professional quality and easy to read. They should display the company's name prominently on the product or service.

To get the pictures made inexpensively or for free, try the following sources:

1) *An architecture firm*: architects are used to doing renderings and can do them quickly. In slow times, they may take on small pro bono (free) projects to keep their draftsmen busy.

2) *A corporation* with in-house design services: ask for an in-kind donation.

3) *Vocational schools, community colleges, or art schools*: renderings of ventures make great student projects.

4) *Ad agencies, design firms and printers*: may do it for a nominal fee as a portfolio piece.

The point of the proposal is not to do a heavy pitch for your venture, but rather to remind your contact about its salient points and to act as a teaser for his boss. The proposal contains no long philosophies. No rationals. No budget. It succinctly paints a picture of your potential partnership's success. It makes the corporation an offer that looks to be a natural, comfortable and valuable fit.

It is a tool to convince the corporation that they want to do business with you, and to get you back in the door to discuss the details of the deal. It should lead to a second meeting at which you discuss how to make the venture best meet both partners' needs and how much it will cost to do.

CHAPTER 26:

Retail Sales

"Once the toothpaste is out of the tube,
it's hard to get it back in."
— H.R. Haldeman,
he met his Watergate

Try everything else first.

Until now this book has talked about wholesaling your products and services through corporations. That way there's a guaranteed sale, minimum cash outlay, no unsold inventory, low risk to you. It's the easiest, safest way to go.

Selling to the general public is risky. It requires a lot of money for manufacturing, warehousing, advertising and selling the inventory — and you have no guarantee the merchandise will sell. You're no longer talking about doing a venture: you're talking about running a business.

You will require the same planning and capital as any start-up business; you'll also face the same risk. U.S. Commerce Department statistics show more than 90% of all new businesses fail within ten years, so we recommend you consider this route only after you have exhausted all preselling methods. If you do decide to retail, here are some things to consider:

1. Write a business plan. Get experts in the field you are entering to help you develop a solid business plan before beginning. The plan will provide an operating path to follow in implementing the business, and will be a tool for raising cash from business partners or financial institutions.

The plan should include four main points:

A **strategic plan** which explains the product or service's role in the marketplace and in the organization, and what its main business objectives will be.

An **operational plan** which explains how the organization plans to implement the business.

A **financial plan** which indicates projected expenses and income.

A **contingency plan** which describes how the organization will handle unexpected events.

Your public library or local business school library will have many books on how to develop a business plan. Consult one of them for more specific information. A business school class might even be willing to develop a plan for you as a class project.

2. Provide adequate capital. The major reason new businesses fail is because they are undercapitalized. Be sure you aren't. When you do your business plan *pro forma,* be conservative. Don't get caught six months into the business without adequate capital to meet the demand.

3. Install a solid management team. The second reason new businesses fail is weak management. Do you have qualified, *experienced* managers to undertake this project? If not, find them. Without them don't do the business.

4. Create "safety net" sales. Even if you're confident about public sales, maximize your product or service's income potential by also selling it as a corporate premium item and/or selling it through a publisher or distributor. Plan to use it in-house as a membership inducement or fundraising premium. The more sales avenues you can create, the less risky the business will be.

5. Negotiate a licensing agreement with a manufacturer. This is the best way to reduce risk, although in exchange you sacrifice revenue. In a licensing agreement, you contract with a manufacturer to produce the product for you, with your name, logo and information on it. The manufacturer also markets it, and gives you a percentage of the sales.

A number of nonprofits have successfully pursued this route:

Children's Television Workshop
Licenses Sesame Street characters to manufacturers of children's clothing and products, and nets several million dollars each year.

The California Grape Board
Earned millions of dollars by licensing their advertising mascots, the California Raisins, to manufacturers of everything from plush toys to radios.

Of course, the trick to licensing is having a product with large enough sales potential to be of interest to a manufacturer. A licensing agent can help connect you with a manufacturer, and help you negotiate the best deal.

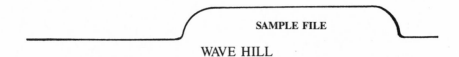

SAMPLE FILE

WAVE HILL

Wave Hill is a nonprofit public garden and cultural institution located in the Bronx, New York. In 1985, Wave Hill wanted to augment their funding, and increase public awareness of the institution and its need for money. Administrators at Wave Hill decided to start a commercial venture selling lawn chairs like those used in their gardens.

The Wave Hill chair is based on the chair designed by architect

Gerrit Rietveld, on display at the Museum of Modern Art. The Wave Hill gardening staff built the chairs specifically for display in the garden, and to be given to donors of large gifts as a premium. Visitors to Wave Hill have admired them since they were first placed in the gardens twenty years ago.

Selling the chairs to the public seemed an excellent way to raise money and promote the organization. The staff had experience manufacturing the chairs and down time during the winter in which to build them. Also, the popularity of the chairs indicated there was a viable market.

The business was operated by a small group of Wave Hill employees and overseen by the Director of Development, who assumed responsibility after the first year of operation. The gardeners on the staff occasionally needed assistance from outside the operation since peak demand for the chair coincided with peak demand for the gardeners' time, Spring and Summer. The chairs were promoted in fliers and press releases that were sent to members, prospective customers and newspapers. The business also received free national coverage in well-known publications such as *The New York Times* and *House Beautiful*. As a result, inquiries came in from people throughout the country.

But there was a major flaw in the business plan — there was no way to distribute the chairs. Shippers, like United Parcel Service, refused to deliver them fully assembled because they were too large. And disassembling the chair, in the opinion of the venture managers, compromised the quality of the product.

The venture managers considered selling the chair through retail outlets, but decided against it because they felt they lost too much control over the product. Retailers wanted to charge prices for the chair the Wave Hill managers considered excessive. They feared this would have a negative impact on the organization's image.

According to Peter Sauer, the Director of Wave Hill, "It was extremely difficult for us to tie into distribution channels because our operation is so small. We have little bargaining power with large companies." Ultimately, the chairs were distributed only in the metropolitan New York City area. They were delivered by members of the gardening staff for a fee, or picked up by customers directly from Wave Hill. Potential customers from outside the New York City area could get the chairs only if they made arrangements to have them delivered. Many sales were lost as a result. Despite their limited distribution, seventy-six chairs were sold in the first two years of the operation and brought in revenue of $9,500. (Profit figures were not available.)

The chair was priced at $125, based on the approximate manufacturing costs. According to one source the price did not cover overhead and supervision, and probably did not cover the full labor cost, as it diverted employees from their work in the gardens.

Now in its third year, the business is still run by the Wave Hill staff, but the product is not actively promoted. Because of the problems they encountered and the unanticipated complexity of the operation, Wave Hill managers decided to search for alternative ways to keep the business alive without being directly involved. An arrangement was negotiated (in early 1988) with a large seed and garden supply company, giving them the license to manufacture and market the chair for royalty fees. The company, which will begin selling the chair (in 1989), has the manufacturing, marketing, and distribution capabilities to successfully run the operation on a large scale.

Despite the problems, Mr. Sauer called the venture "an unqualified success. It achieved the objectives set at the start of the venture, that is, to generate income for the organization, and increase public awareness of Wave Hill."

As the venture managers at Wave Hill learned, it is vital to consider all aspects of marketing before commencing a venture. A great product and proven demand were not enough to assure the venture's success — *they also needed a way to get the product to the customer.* A marketing plan, its sophistication determined by the complexity of the venture, is essential to determine whether or not the organization has the resources, expertise, systems, and philosophy to make the venture a success.[6]

CHAPTER 27:

New Markets For Your Existing Programs

"As pretty as you are,
you know you could have been a flower;
If good looks was a minute,
you know that you could be an hour;
The way you stole my heart,
you know you could have been a cool crook;
And baby you're so smart,
you know you could have been a school book."
— The Way You Do The Things You Do[7]

The Primes had an interesting sound. They just needed a little repackaging. They donned coordinated white, sequined outfits and added some smooth choreography to their act. Repackaged, they sold 22 million records worldwide and became one of the most successful rhythm and blues groups of all time: The Temptations. *The Way You Do The Things You Do*, the anthem of repackaging, was their first hit.

Before you start thinking about developing new products, services or special events, take a good look at what you already have. Chances are your assets include several unsung hits just waiting to be heard. Don't sit on them. Whether they are physical or programmatic, repackage your assets for sale.

GETTING A HIGHER PRICE

Look at the programs you're now offering to a low-paying or non-paying audience. Ask yourself who else might need or want them. Perhaps "Robin Hood Marketing" is in order. Can you sell those same programs at higher prices to more affluent markets?

Vancouver Family Services was already doing counseling for low-income people. To increase their revenue and reach new populations they contracted with corporations to provide the same service to employees.

SAMPLE FILE

IMPACT HOUSE

Impact House, a substance abuse agency in Pasadena, California, provides counseling and treatment for people with drug and alcohol problems. It is funded primarily by government contracts which don't pay the full cost of treatment. However, Impact House has begun offering the same services to corporations. Lockheed, Xerox, Pacific Bell and other major employers pay Impact House up to $350 per day to counsel employees with drug and alcohol problems. The income has insured Impact House's financial stability.

REPACKAGING

Above, the nonprofit took a service it was already performing and sold it, unchanged, to a new, more affluent market. However sometimes a sale to a new market requires repackaging and "repositioning" the product or service in order to better meet the new market's need.

SAMPLE FILE

BRONX FRONTIER DEVELOPMENT CORPORATION

The Bronx Frontier Development Corporation is a neighborhood self-help agency. Through neighborhood improvement projects it creates jobs. One of its projects was a community farm which grew and sold spices to hotels, cruise ships and restaurants. The highest fixed expense of the farm was fertilizer, so in an attempt to cut costs, Frontier collected free manure from the Bronx Zoo. (For the Zoo this was a great waste management solution.) The manure made excellent fertilizer, and before long, other neighborhood gardeners were asking if they could have some too. So the enterprising Frontier packaged "Zoo Doo" as a deluxe fertilizer for house plants and gardens. The clever packaging caught the eye of Bloomingdale's where it sold 30,000 bags annually in catalog sales. Frontier has licensed the name to zoos around the country and makes royalties off their sales.

SAMPLE FILE

CENTER IN THE PARK

The Center in the Park, a senior service center in Philadelphia, offers low-cost field trips to its clients. The trips are highly popular, and the center frequently has to turn people away. To decrease demand for the trips – and to make money on them without increasing the charge to clients – the Center created a CIP (Center in the Park) Card and repositioned the trips as a benefit for cardholders. The card, which costs $5, grossed $5,000 in its first few weeks.

SAMPLE FILE

DALLAS CLASSICAL GUITAR SOCIETY

The Dallas Classical Guitar Society wanted to sell tapes of classical guitar music. To broaden their appeal, they positioned them as "romantic – music for spending time with that special person." They packaged the tapes with a bottle of wine, two glasses and a rose, and named the new product "Romance in a Box." They use the boxes as high-end membership premiums and wholesale them to liquor stores.

TAPPING PHYSICAL ASSETS

When your machines are turned off, what else could they be doing? When a space is empty, how could it be filled?

Take a hard look at your physical assets to see if any can be used to generate revenue.

SAMPLE FILE

GREAT FALLS HOSPITAL

It's hard to believe that a hospital cafeteria could be known for good food, but that's the case at the Great Falls Hospital in Montana. The cafeteria also had down times between meal services when they could prepare extra food. So hospital administrators decided to capitalize on their asset. They opened a catering service, first catering just staff parties, and now expanding to community functions.

SAMPLE FILE

SACRAMENTO ARTS COMMISSION

Like most other nonprofits, the Sacramento Arts Commission has a phone machine which gives information about its programs and services. Unlike most others, it rents time on its line to local arts groups who use it to advertise their upcoming performances. In one stroke, the Arts Commission is performing its arts advocacy function and generating income!

SAMPLE FILE

WQED RADIO

WQED, the Pittsburgh public radio station, has a large library of classical and jazz tapes which it taps as a revenue source. For a fee, WQED will provide customized music for weddings, parties or other events. They've even been contracted by the city transit authority to package music for the new city subway system.

SEEING YOUR AUDIENCE FROM ALL SIDES

One of the most valuable but overlooked assets in a nonprofit is its audience. Most organizations contact thousands of people a year – users, donors, suppliers and colleagues. Yet they miss their potential as income generators.

What most nonprofits fail to realize is that your current audience is your best audience. They're easy to reach, and they're ready to buy. It pays to give them plenty of chances.

You can do this by thinking of your audience as a rectangle. Before you jump to conclusions, hear us out. Most people will come to your organization in one of four ways:

1) As members
2) As donors
3) As buyers (of a product or service) or
4) As visitors (to a special event)

Too often, nonprofits isolate these groups. Donors are invited to certain events, members to others, and the general public to yet others. The groups are treated as if they were eligible for only one type of relationship with the organization. They're not!

Your real job is to try to win each group over into the other three categories. If you think of each of these "entry" points as the corner of a rectangle, your job is to slide everybody around to the other three corners.

visitors		members
buyers		donors

First make sure each of the "entry" experiences is positive so everyone will want to come back. Then give them regular and appealing opportunities to do so. Create a varied menu of opportunities to associate with you throughout the year, including chances to buy products or services, invitations to attend events, opportunities to join, and requests for donations.

Then make sure everyone in all four categories is invited to everything. To do this, you'll have to capture complete names and addresses of every contact. Log them on a computerized database that can sort by type of contact (donor, member, etc.) and merge lists. Then mail materials to all your contacts at least three times a year.

SAMPLE FILE

THE NATIONAL GEOGRAPHIC SOCIETY

The National Geographic Society is a master at this. Their magazine reaches millions of people who pay $18 a year to read about the world around them. But why just read about it? National Geographic goes back to those subscribers with games, calendars, videotapes, a children's magazine and other items – all spin-offs of their basic product.

SAMPLE FILE

MINNESOTA PUBLIC RADIO

Minnesota Public Radio has done the same thing a different way. They are the folks who brought you "A Prairie Home Companion," and they knew a loyal audience when they heard one. They tapped their audience with an annual catalog of Prairie Home Companion merchandise.

The catalog operation has expanded considerably from its early days when boxes of T-shirts bulged from under desks. It's become a for-profit subsidiary, the Riverton Trading Company, with an annual gross of $9 million. Their database of 55,000 buyers is attractive to advertisers, so MPR launched a magazine which generates ad revenue.

They've recently tapped their audience one more time by starting a consulting service which helps other public media stations start catalog operations. All this from recognizing the potential in their local family of subscribers.

ACCESSING YOUR NETWORK

Equally as important as your users, may be your peer organizations. What networks are you in? To whom do you have access? By networking other organizations you may be able to create a purchasing group with a lot of clout.

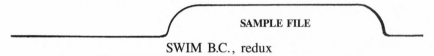

SAMPLE FILE

SWIM B.C., redux

Swim B.C. is the Canadian nonprofit that promotes recreational and competitive swimming. Its single center in Vancouver serves several hundred thousand people annually — a respectable number, but peanuts compared to the seven million Canadians who swim recreationally each year. How to reach those seven million? How to capitalize on their interest in swimming? Swim B.C. is organizing other centers across Canada to create a national network of swim centers.

Through the network, they'll have access to millions of Canadian swimmers to whom they'll market a private line of merchandise called "Otterwear." The products will be sold in "aquatic boutiques" in each center, through a mail-order catalog, and retail. A portion of each sale will go to Swim B.C. and a portion will stay with the center that made the sale.

OPTIMIZING YOUR BUILDING AND GROUNDS

Another valuable asset may be your building and/or grounds. Whose needs can they meet beside your own? Are there long hours when you're not in your building? Are there groups in town that need rehearsal space? Meeting space? Party space? Classroom space?

Space and ground rental can be an easy, low-cost way to generate income. Just make sure you've covered all your costs in making the space available — heat, lights, staff, security, insurance, etc., plus a profit — before you sign a lease.

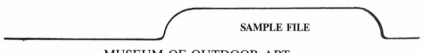

SAMPLE FILE

MUSEUM OF OUTDOOR ART

Given the nature of its collection, it's not surprising that the Museum of Outdoor Art in Greenwood Village, Colorado has a lot of land. What is surprising is the way they've used it to generate income. A section of the property forms a natural ampitheater and the Museum had, from time to time, rented the area to the Denver Symphony and other groups for staging concerts. But the rentals were sporadic and the income inconsistent.

When a friend of the Museum's attended an entertainment promoters conference and heard that the developing trend among concert promoters was to rent alternative, non-auditorium-style arenas, the Museum realized they were literally sitting on a gold mine. They contacted MCA, the entertainment conglomerate which organizes national concert tours, and proposed their site as the Denver setting for a season's concerts.

MCA liked the idea. They gave the Museum money to co-develop the site with seating and a professional stage, and the two organizations signed a lucrative contract for several seasons of big name rock, folk and jazz concerts. Now in the third year of the partnership, the Museum has expanded the venture by joining with a nearby Hyatt Hotel to offer a concert/hotel package. Buyers receive discount hotel accommodations with their concert ticket, and the Museum gets a percentage of each sale.

SAMPLE FILE

HISTORIC DENVER

Historic Denver, the city's historic preservation organization, owns and operates the Molly Brown House, home of the unsinkable Victorian hostess. One of the strategies that keeps Historic Denver afloat is space rentals in Molly's house.

The organization rents out the third floor ballroom for Victorian dinners, lunches and high teas. The food, authentic dishes from turn of the century Denver, is served by volunteers wearing reproduction costumes from the period, amidst authentic table decorations and period furnishings. Meals can seat up to 40 people who pay $50 per person for the dinners (lunches and teas are less). The fee includes a tour of the House and a brief background on Victorian society.

Amazingly, the entire operation is run by volunteers under the supervision of the Molly Brown House director. The 15 volunteers who organize, cook and serve the meals are all on three-year contracts with the organization. At the rate of one meal every other week, they are barely able to keep up with demand, so Historic Denver is considering contracting the service to a caterer in order to accommodate more parties.

For the organization, the meals offer a steady income, especially during the winter when the House serves fewer tourists. They also provide a popular and engaging way to teach Denver history. The organization also rents the ballroom without the meals, but fewer people select that option. Renters prefer the elegant parties and the authentic Victorian atmosphere they provide. After all, that's what visiting the Molly Brown House is all about.

"BUNDLING" PROGRAMS

Robert Carr and Johnny Mitchell, two Bronx, New York teenagers, had been singing solo without much success. But when they harmonized together, they sounded great. Together, they spent 22 weeks on the national music charts with the 1958 "bundling" classic, *We Belong Together*.

There are times when you can increase the salability of your products and services by "bundling" two or more together. Each benefits from the added value of the other. Appropriately, we call this the "Robert & Johnny Effect."

SAMPLE FILE

KCFR RADIO

KCFR, the public radio station in Denver, used bundling to package its summer concert series. They knew their listeners would enjoy live jazz and classical concerts, but they had no facility in which to hold them. They could have rented a local concert hall, but that didn't add sizzle to the event. Instead, they "bundled" their concerts with the attractive outdoor amphitheater of the Denver Botanic Garden, and the result is one of the most popular summer events in the city. Tickets to the annual series of outdoor concerts are usually sold out within hours of going on sale.

SAMPLE FILE

ROCKY MOUNTAIN INSTITUTE

The Rocky Mountain Institute used "bundling" to create a whole new way to sell their services. RMI does research and consulting on economic renewal. They offer a variety of services designed to revitalize communities by strengthening local business. Sold separately, the services were slow movers.

So RMI bundled their services into a package called "Competitek." A Competitek package has a fixed price, lasts exactly one year, and offers an attractive "blend" of services. The combined services offer a comprehensive solution to a community's economic problems, making the package more desirable. As a result, packaged services now generate a substantial portion of RMI's income. An added benefit to RMI is their efficiency. Whereas before RMI staff spent a lot of time pushing many small sales, they now make fewer sales that pay off bigger.

CHAPTER 28:

Making The Promise Real

"The whole idea is to deliver what money can't buy."
—Bruce Springsteen,
idol

TALL TIMBERS TO TOOTHPICKS, THE DUMMY DOESN'T LAST LONG

Edgar Bergen and Charley McCarthy were stars on radio but with the advent of TV they faded. Was it because Edgar was the kind of ventriloquist who needed radio to gloss over his moving lips? The point is, once you're out in the open with a promise, you've got to perform.

In creating a vision for your organization, you've made a promise — to yourselves, to your investors and to your publics. You've told them where you're going in the next few years, what you plan to achieve, and some of the paths you will take to get there. Now you have to make that promise real. You have to give people concrete evidence that you're doing what you said you would.

Each of your products, services and special events is a realization of the promise. Each one should demonstrate to the public that you are moving toward your goals. The Denver Children's Museum "promised" to provide high quality educational products and services for families, and followed through with publications, traveling exhibits and special events that encouraged families to play and learn together. The National Crime Prevention Council "promised" to help America take a bite out of crime, and followed through with print materials, media campaigns, and community and corporate action kits that give citizens the tools for fighting crime in their worksites, homes and neighborhoods.

Each of your products, services and special events should do the same for you. Each one should be directly related to the vision you created. Each should be one more demonstration that you are making that promise real.

STANDIN' BY YOUR CANON

Your promise doesn't stop there. You've also promised your public that you would be customer-centered and that you would be the best organization in your area of specialty. Now you have to look for ways to realize those goals. Swope Health Center wanted to realize its promise to be "the best health clinic for modest-income people," so they repainted the stripes in their parking lot. They painted "staff only" green stripes far away from the door, reserving the close-in spaces for patients. It was a literal way of saying to patients, "You come first."

Look at all the places in your organization where customer contact happens — at your front counter, in your billing operation, as well as in the delivery of your primary service. Are all those contacts making your promise real?

You've segmented your audience in order to meet individual group's needs. Now look at your organization from each group's point of view. Do you say you want Spanish-speaking customers, but post signs only in English? Do you say you want families at your programs, but offer most of your programs on weekdays? Look at all the messages your organization puts out — implicit as well as explicit. What promises are you making, and what are you really delivering?

The same kind of scrutiny should be applied to every communication that travels out your front door. Everything you send into the world is a complete picture of your organization to the person who sees it — from business letters to your van on the highway. For some people, that one communication may be the only "message" they ever see! So make it count. Make sure every contact is an accurate, engineered reflection of your organization. Make each convey the promise you've made to the public — to be the best organization in your field.

Print materials are as important as activities. If you can't make it top quality, don't do it. Too often, nonprofits confuse slick with professional. They fear that expensive-looking print pieces will make them look too well endowed to attract funds. Freeze that assumption! Poverty doesn't sell; professionalism does. Each piece must remind the public that you're making your quality promise real.

KEEPING YOUR CONTACT VISCERAL

Part of making the promise real is communicating. It's not enough to offer quality products and services. You have to tell consumers you're doing it. It's not enough to improve the quality of customer contact. You have to tell potential customers about it. As you strengthen your ability to make good on your promises, take every opportunity to spread that message.

To do that effectively and inexpensively, ask each of your corporate partners to advertise your ventures in their own ads, mailers and newsletters. It strengthens their association with you, and lets you reach broad audiences for free. Ask corporations that have shied away from joint ventures with you, to include information about you in their mailers. They will gain some of the benefit of a joint venture without the expense. Ask grocery stores to print messages from you on their paper bags. They will benefit from the association; you will reach thousands of people with discount coupons (for products, services or special events), with half-price membership offers, or with some other organizational message.

In a sense, once you become an entrepreneurial, customer-centered organization, every contact with the public becomes an inducement, a reason to get closer to you — a chance for a sale, now or in the future. Each contact should remind them how you can meet their needs.

 Once you become an entrepreneurial organization, every contact with the public becomes a chance for a sale.

 If you can't make it top quality, don't do it.

CHAPTER 29:

A Timeline

"We know that as a people,
we must seize our time."
  —Bobby Seale,
    Black Panther, Chicago 8, barbecue cookbook author

"My protest days are over."
  —Jerry Rubin,
    Yippie, Chicago 8, nightclub party producer

"I was political then,
I'm political now."
  —Lee Weiner,
    Sociology teacher, Chicago 8, nonprofit entrepreneur

How long should this whole process take? From the time you become serious about enterprise and administer the questionnaire, to the time you start pitching your first venture to a corporation, should take about 90 days. Once you start, it's important to keep the momentum going.

By the end of 30 days you should have completed your vision and should have strong visuals and a slogan ready to show potential corporate partners.

By the end of 60 days you should have narrowed your list of possible ventures to the top three first choices, and you should be checking those three against the 9 Criteria.

By the end of 90 days you should have selected your first venture, you should have its proposal ready and you should be making appointments with corporate decision makers to pitch it.

It's not long from there until your first venture is operational and you're planning Number Two. By now you should be viewing everything with an entrepreneurial eye.

That's an ambitious schedule, but enterprise is a fast-paced game. If you can't move quickly now, you'll have a hard time keeping up later. Within three to five years, your old, pre-entrepreneurial organization should be just a memory to you, your audiences and your community.

PART V

Vehicles: Driving
The Fantasy
Home

CHAPTER 30:

Introducing Enterprise Into Your Organization

You've created a vision of an entrepreneurial organization. You've developed ideas for ventures the organization can do. This part of our book will give you the vehicles for implementing both. You've done the hard, creative work. This is the mechanics, the systems and structures that will help you integrate enterprise smoothly into your organization.

***

WELCOME TO THE NEW WORLD

In 1928, according to Gary Cooper, he and actress Nancy Carroll were shooting the last scenes of *The Shopworn Angel* for Paramount Pictures when, for the first time, sound was available to filmakers. Paramount wanted to be part of the new technology immediately. So a bit of dialogue was added. "I studied my script containing this new thing called dialogue," Cooper told the *Saturday Evening Post*, "until it was letter perfect." In the film's closing seconds, a wedding scene, the first and only words were uttered:

> Cooper: *"I do."*
> Carroll: *"I do."*

With those four words the picture was released as a talkie, seizing the opportunity to grow with the times.

LOW COMMOTION

If your organization is like most nonprofits, it won't be used to entrepreneurial behaviors. You'll be asking people who are used to reacting to customers' demands to proactively seek out those customers' needs. You may be asking a system that is used to concensus decision-making to streamline its own inefficient-but-comfortable process. Most difficult of all, you will be asking an organization that thinks solely about service to start thinking about making money.

None of these behaviors will come quickly or easily. You are asking people to accept some fundamental changes in the way their organization runs, and change is

177

frightening. They will need to be educated honestly about the new direction and why it's happening, and treated patiently as they learn the new behaviors.

It helps to recognize that this is not the first time your organization has changed. Organizations go through many stages as they grow — from infancy to adolescence to maturity. At each stage people leave because the organization is no longer the one they chose to work in. The introduction of enterprise is one more stage. For some staff it will be a natural progression. They will adapt readily, they will relish the change. Others may never accept it. Let them go. They will be happier in a more traditional nonprofit.

THE FEAR THAT BLINDS

The greatest fear in organizations that turn to enterprise is that quality will be sacrificed for money. Staffs fear that the organization will lose its mission in its desire to earn money, that money will become an end in itself, rather than merely a means to get there. Recognize this fear and address it. It is a fear that often is seen and manifested in political infighting. Beware! Encourage people to express their concern so it doesn't fester underground. Then patiently explain your own concern for quality.

Plan to spend a lot of time educating your staff about enterprise. Just as you need to actively communicate your changes to the outside world, you need to do "internal marketing" with your staff and board. Remind them how enterprise furthers the organization's mission, about how it enables you to reach new audiences, how it earns money to subsidize programs that won't pay for themselves.

Assure them that money will be a means to an end, never an end in itself. Assure them that you won't sacrifice quality for money, that the quality of programs will be nonnegotiable. The people who create programs now should be among the designers and implementers of your new programs; they should see those programs as furthering what they do now. They must work closely with enterprise staff to set goals and standards. They must be your voices of quality control.

PREDICTABLE PROBLEMS

There will be some tension between your programs and enterprise staffs. That is unavoidable. Programs staff will push for programs the enterprise staff can't sell. That's okay: pursue your traditional sources of funding for those. Enterprise staff will push for some projects your programs staff dislikes. That is also okay, let them battle it out. The debates between them are healthy! They will force you to constantly reexamine your goals and your means of achieving them. Because of this tension, entrepreneurial organizations are dynamic places. They never become rusty or out of touch with their audiences. Their missions and visions don't get locked in bottom drawers. They never become complacent.

Tensions only become a problem when they are underground, so be sensitive to them. Watch for people who consistently make trouble. Some longtime staffers may be unwilling to adjust to the changes, yet unwilling to leave the organization. They may rebel against the organization by instigating political infighting. Be aware of it. Don't let it continue. Staff people who cannot make peace with the new ways can poison the organization. You may be faced with the difficult decision of terminating someone who has been a valuable member of the staff, but if your organization is serious about its new direction, don't hesitate. Both the organization and the individual will be better off.

TEAM RESOLVE

If you take seriously your job of educating the staff, you should find the acceptance level high. Enterprise is an exciting process! It can bring you closer to your goals than you ever hoped. Most organizations that choose this route find it a unifying factor for their staffs; people are galvanized by the vision and become eager to implement it. They find that as they decide which corporations to work with and which to avoid, which ventures to pursue and which to refuse, not everyone agrees with every decision. But everyone believes in the organization's commitment to enterprise and, thus, its commitment to its mission.

SAMPLE FILE

ONTARIO SCIENCE CENTER

The Ontario Science Center in Toronto has long been a leader in the development of interactive science exhibits. As such, they receive frequent requests to develop exhibits for other centers. Recognizing the potential, and faced with the prospect of declining government subsidies, the Center decided to pursue exhibit development and fabrication as an income generating activity.

For their initial venture, they chose to market a set of topology puzzles which are extremely popular at the Center. Each puzzle has two to four clear acrylic pieces held together with rope. As the puzzler tries to separate the plastic pieces by twisting and sliding them around each other, he explores the relationship of surfaces that forms the basis of topology. Science Center staff had manufactured the puzzle pieces that were used at the Center. But when they investigated commercial fabrication of the pieces, a puzzle of a different kind surfaced.

The Science Center puzzles contained several cylindrical parts. To have those pieces manufactured commercially would be quite expensive. Cheaper, and equally serviceable, would be to manufacture each cylindrical piece as a flat shape. The Center commissioned a trial set of puzzles with the new flattened shapes and when they came back from the manufacturer, the staff was unhappy. The puzzles still accomplished their purpose, although they had lost the satisfying feeling of holding a cool, smooth, acrylic cylinder in the palm of your hand. The puzzles still worked, but they had lost their aesthetic. .

What to do? On the one hand, to realize the largest possible profit margin, the Center wanted the lowest possible fabrication cost. On the other hand, they were committed to the quality of their product. After much debate, they chose the more expensive cylinders. They felt the puzzle had to represent the Science Center to the world and, therefore, had to be up to their usual standard. In fact, they decided, the increased quality would enhance sales. They willingly shrank their profit margin for the sake of quality.

CHAPTER 31:

Creating A Department Of Enterprise

*"Bureaucracy defends the status quo
long past the time when the quo has lost its status."*
—Laurence Peter,
of the Peter Principle

CLOGGED FUEL LINES

Every day in the U.S. the federal government issues another 100 pages of rules and regulations, while in the same day, six million tons of manure hit the ground behind farm animals.[7] Make of that what you will and trust your animal instincts; don't let yourself get clogged or bloated with bureaucracy. No matter how excited you are about enterprise, your organization harbors a lifetime of non-entrepreneurial habits. To succeed, your ventures must be sheltered from them. Ventures must be given protection by the Executive Director, and freedom to be different from other organizational projects.

Ventures need distance from some of the operating rules of the organization, yet they need intimacy with others. The ventures will be furthering your mission. They will convey your spirit, philosophy and quality. They will rely on your staff for quality checks, program support and advice. Achieving this balance between distance and closeness is one of the primary challenges of introducing enterprise to your organization.

INDEPENDENT SUSPENSION

Start by installing a Department of Enterprise or a Department of Marketing on a par with your other major departments or divisions. Have it report to the Executive Director or Chief Administrator, and make its director part of the top management team. That way it has room to maneuver somewhat independently, yet is tied to your other departments and has a clear position in the organization's hierarchy.

Then allow the department to create its own rules. It will need to be more responsive to external demands than your organization is used to being, so it will need the freedom and resources to respond quickly and successfully.

Keep the following in mind as you install your Department of Enterprise:

Don't tie the department down to the same layers of decision-making that exist elsewhere in your organization. Unnecessary people get into the process, they bog it down. Enterprise demands streamlined decisions, not the "tyranny of democracy."

Let the department hire and fire its own staff. The Director of Enterprise will have a better sense of the skills he needs than someone used to hiring for a non-profit. Give him the freedom to hire the skills he needs.

Let the department recommend its own system of salary incentives and rewards. The salary issue is a tricky one. Enterprise staff may need to be hired from the private sector where they are accustomed to higher salaries than you currently pay. This naturally causes resentment in other staff. While there is no way to eliminate this conflict immediately, there are some things you can do to mitigate it:

• Use a system of incentives and rewards to compensate enterprise staff for accepting lower salaries than they are used to making.

• Use the introduction of enterprise and its resulting earned income to raise all salaries to higher levels.

• Offer all staff the opportunity to increase earnings with a system of incentives and rewards (see Chapter 33).

Let the department control its own cash flow. The department will need access to cash irregularly and immediately. Make that possible for the department to do so.

SUBSIDIARY INSULATION

Creating a department that operates differently from others in the organization is not easy. It places a great deal of responsibility on the Executive Director to justify the differences, and to minimize resentment between the enterprise department and others. For this reason, some organizations choose to incorporate their departments of enterprise as nonprofit subsidiaries. This makes it structurally easier to create different rules for the division. It also has several other advantages. It insulates your organization from liability should a venture turn sour. It protects your nonprofit status if the enterprise activity is deemed unrelated to your mission. And a separate for-profit-minded subsidiary may more easily attract corporate partners.

The subsidiary can be nonprofit or for-profit, depending on the types of ventures it plans to do. Small ventures directly related to your mission are best handled in a nonprofit corporation. Larger, ongoing, less closely related ventures should be handled by a for-profit. Consult a tax attorney who is familiar with nonprofit enterprise if you are considering pursuing this route.

The concern in creating a subsidiary is that it become too removed from the mission, spirit, and service-oriented nature of the organization. If subsidiary staff are not functionally part of the organization, if they don't interact daily with the organization's staff, will they be able to implement projects that reflect the organization's integrity and quality?

There is no right or wrong answer to this question. Each organization must choose the path that fits it best. Whichever route you choose, treat your new department with care. It takes a lot less to kill a new effort than to nourish it, and enterprise will seem more foreign and risky than most. Nurture it all you can.

CHAPTER 32:

Staffing The Department Of Enterprise

"Said the Queen, 'Now here, you see,
it takes all the running you can do
to keep in the same place.
If you want to get somewhere else,
you must run at least twice as fast as that!' "
– Charles "Lewis Carroll" Dodgson,
Through the Looking Glass

"Staff a new department?!" you say, "Now you're really talking fantasy. We can't afford that!" Relax.

Initially all you need in a Department of Enterprise is a director. He or she can work closely with the chief administrator and programs staff to conceive ventures and sell them. Once they're sold, he can hire contract staff to implement them. You don't need to hire additional staff until the work for the department has outgrown the director's time constraints.

A DIRECTOR: THE ART OF THE KEEL

Hiring the director, however, is critical. For enterprise to succeed, the department must have a full-time (or very close to full-time) champion, a captain who gives the department backbone and direction; someone whose primary responsibility is to sell ventures and see them through implementation. If you give the job to someone wearing another hat, the job won't get properly done. Enterprise demands a different outlook, a different set of skills than anyone in your organization may be currently using. To ask someone to do his existing, traditional job plus this new and different one is unfair and unrealistic.

The person you're looking for may already be on staff. If you've designated an Enterprise Champion, that person is most likely your candidate. If so, peel off his other responsibilities so he can concentrate on enterprise. In some organizations the Executive Director functions as the director of enterprise. This may work for a short time, while the process is just being launched, but once the work demands serious concentration and special skills, most Executive Directors find it necessary to hire someone else. Sometimes delaying your decision can take the organization dangerously off course, severely hampering the organization.

When you hire a Director of Enterprise, what qualities should you look for? You need someone with a foot in both camps, nonprofit and for-profit; someone who will love and honor your mission, at the same time that he understands the bottom line and thinks like a business person. Not an easy person to find – but possible!

First and foremost, look for someone who understands and values your mission. Your director will need to promote that mission in every venture, so he has to believe in it wholeheartedly. Second, look for someone who is familiar with business and can apply business principles to a nonprofit. Third, look for someone who enjoys sales. Half the director's job will be creative: conceiving ventures, looking for partnership opportunities, working with staff to find ways the organization can tap market opportunities. The other half will be sales: cold calls and follow-up sales calls to get your ventures sold. This second half is important. You need to hire someone who genuinely likes selling, who isn't a programs person waiting for the right job to open.

15 CAPTAIN QUALITIES

Qualities to look for in your Director of Enterprise:

1. Oriented toward sales, not public relations. PR people leave a meeting wanting everyone to feel good. Sales people leave a meeting knowing quantities, prices and delivery dates.

2. Tolerance for ambiguity. Sales involves indecision, competing interests and shifting priorities. It's not for someone who needs one right answer and wants it right away.

3. Willingness to risk failure and rejection. You'll never make every sale. Just learn from every experience.

4. Strong organizational skills. Sales people have their fingers in a lot of pots. They're constantly scouting the marketplace, prospecting leads, tracking past leads and clients, following up contacts, and working with suppliers to understand and deliver the product or service. It takes someone well organized and systematic.

5. Integrity. Your sales person should love your organization and its mission; should understand and believe in what he or she sells; and should promise only what the organization can deliver.

6. Enthusiasm. Enthusiasm is infectious. It will be one of his or her strongest sales tool.

7. Enjoys solving problems. Sales is really a problem-solving exercise. It involves listening to a corporation's problems and looking for ways your organization's expertise or creativity can meet them.

8. Optimism. Good sales people see opportunities where others see problems. They tend to be upbeat and positive.

9. Resourcefulness. Sales requires the ability to think quickly on your feet. Look for someone who's a creative thinker.

10. Sense of humor. Laughter can lighten the tensest meeting, and can see someone through when the "no's" seem overwhelming.

11. Ability to listen. If you're going to match your product or service with a corporation's need, you better listen well to the need. Good sales people know that the more they listen, the smarter they look.

12. Genuinely likes people. When it comes right down to it, sales is relationships between people. People buy from people, not from institutions. If you like people, it shows.

13. Articulate. Look for someone who can explain your vision clearly and without jargon.

14. High energy level. You need someone action-oriented, eager to make the next call, and willing to try again after rejection; someone who can maintain a sometimes grueling level of activity without becoming unreasonably grumpy.

15. Competitive. Good sales people are mildly impatient. They want results and try not to let it show . . . too much!

NAVIGATING RELATIONSHIPS

If your board is reluctant to create a new position, hire the Director of Enterprise on contract. If you're hiring someone new to the organization, this will give you both a chance to test the waters. It may also make it easier to hire the best person for the job, since the right candidate may have other commitments to fulfill before joining you full-time and long-term. Remember, though, no flirting with enterprise! Your commitment to the strategy must be long-term even if the initial contract isn't.

Consider making the contract "no cut." That is, include a clause that says the director can't be fired if his first (or even first few) ventures fail. He'll need some room to take risks, and he won't have it if he's worried about losing his job to a failure. Consider including that clause in the Executive Director's contract as well. Especially if your board is nervous about enterprise, the added security will bolster your willingness to experiment and strengthen your ventures.

What is the relationship between the Director of Enterprise and the Executive Director? One of trust! You hire someone who understands your values and goals, who shares your vision, and has the skills to implement it entrepreneurially. Then you let him or her go. That doesn't mean you turn your back and stop asking questions. It means you don't try to control the division's operations. As with leadership, you give direction but not directions. You provide a "spiritual check" for the Enterprise Director's activities, but you recognize that some of the means to the end may not be ones you would choose. After all, this business is probably new to you too.

THE CREW

While your department needs only a director initially, your ventures will require additional staff. Some may require skills you have in-house; others may require new ones. Some may need publications expertise; others special events experience. Some may require professional qualifications; others may just need common sense. Don't lock yourself into needing a particular set of skills just because you have a person with those skills on staff. Don't pay high salaries for a year when you only need the skills for a month. And don't pay benefits when you don't need to at all.

Hire people on contract. Hire exactly the skills you need for as long as you need them. Go to the top of each field and hire the best people for the job. Don't forget that it was you who created a vision that says you are the best organization in your field. Now use the best people around to help you prove it.

Whatever you do, don't believe that you can't afford top quality people. That's the old nonprofit way of thinking — that second-class mindset. You can afford them: experienced, high-priced professionals frequently do the job in half the time of their lower-cost colleagues. Also, you're looking at a short-term contract, not a long-term salary. Write their professional costs into the venture's sales price. If you still feel you can't afford professionals, offer them equity shares in your venture; when the project sells, they collect a percentage of the sale. Remember: if you're the best in your field, you attract the best in others. Find creative ways to produce the excellence you promised.

FLAGS

More and more, nonprofits are giving conventional business titles to their staff positions. This is a good idea. It immediately communicates to your corporate contacts what your job levels and responsibilities are, and it's one more way to wave your message of "we mean business." Consider using these terms in place of traditional ones:

NONPROFIT TITLE	CORPORATE EQUIVALENT
Executive Director, Managing Director	President/Chief Executive Officer (CEO)
(Marketing) Director	Vice President for (Marketing)
President of the Board	Chairman of the Board
Vice President of the Board	Vice Chairman of the Board

CHAPTER 33:

Enterprise Instigators

"That power, which erring men call Chance."
—John Milton,
Paradise Lost and Found

RETURN OF THE HICKEY

Remember when you used to take chances? Luck had very little to do with it. There was the thrill of pushing your own expectations, then there was the genuine satisfaction as you accomplished beyond accepted limits. As with the mythic hickey of high school — wherein you proved your desirability without losing physical or emotional sanctity — you are now once again in a position to make your mark.

Unfortunately, nonprofits are traditional old biddies who subscribe (we would like to hope unwittingly) to a host of counterproductive operating assumptions. Most of these bromides sound so "normal." In fact, they have become bloody endemic; you never think to question them! Salaries are low; people burn out; money doesn't have to be generated in our department. That's the way life is in a nonprofit, dear.

Phooey! Good fortune must be sought. That's why entrepreneurial nonprofits are challenging these assumptions, and as a result, have found ways to replace the traditional behaviors with new, more productive ones. Here are some of the enterprise behaviors these progressive nonprofits are using. Adopting them will help you cultivate enterprise thinking in your staff, and will speed your return to the ranks of the risk-takers.

ATTITUDES ABOUT MONEY

Typically, nonprofit staffs don't think in terms of making and saving money. Each department is given a budget — and spends it. No attention is given to making money except in the departments directly responsible for bringing it in, and attention to cost-cutting occurs only at the end of the fiscal year in a last-ditch effort to end the year in the black.

Even at budget planning time, there are no incentives to make or save money. In most nonprofits, the new budget for each department starts from zero, as if it were its first year of operation. Money saved or earned the year before is forgotten. Collective amnesia sets in. Doesn't provide much incentive to make money or save it, does it?

Change this way of thinking by creating incentives for departments to make and save money.

Create a departmental "Enterprise Fund." If a department shows a surplus at the end of the year, let them keep 50% of it for their own discretionary use.

Create an organization-wide profit-sharing plan. Provide an incentive for all staff to make and save money by creating an organization-wide profit-sharing plan. Take a predetermined percentage of the net profit at the end of the year and distribute it to staff based on time worked. Full-time employees get a full share, half-time employees a half share. The plan will also emphasize that all departments work toward overall organizational success, and will partially offset low staff salaries.

BREAKING OLD HABITS

Too often, nonprofit people get in the habit of doing things the same old way. The problems never seem to change, neither do the solutions. This complacency makes it difficult to see changes in your markets, makes it difficult to institute new programs, makes it almost impossible to take risks. Not only is this anti-entrepreneurial thinking, it fosters lassitude and burnout in your staff. Instead, you need to actively promote creative thinking and risk-taking; make it safe to do so.

Institute "Creativity Awards." Charles House, an engineer at Hewlett Packard, won H-P's "Medal of Defiance" by pursuing an idea for an advanced picture tube – despite a kill order from management! Create your own version of the defiance award to actively encourage staff to try new things.

Designate a "Problem of the Month." Each month publicize an organizational problem that's looking for a solution (perhaps an area in which you would like to cut costs or generate additional revenue). Ask employees to offer two bold, imaginative solutions – one that would cost money and one that would not. Offer a prize for the winning solution: dinner for two for a non-monetary solution, half the first year's savings or earnings for one that makes or saves money.

COMPETITIVE SALARIES AND REWARDS

One of the most valuable benefits of enterprise is that it provides unrestricted operating cash which can go toward raising salaries. Your goal should be to offer salaries competitive with the private sector. Announce that to the staff, and as enterprise makes it possible, institute across-the-board annual raises.

In the meantime, supplement salaries with a variety of institutional benefits.

Offer interest-free loans. Staff members may occasionally need small loans for short-term, transitional expenses. Bank loans are expensive and sometimes difficult to get. Create a staff loan policy which will provide small, 30 to 90 day loans, no questions asked.

Offer annual bonuses. Once a year, offer small bonuses to each employee. The amount may be negligible, but the impression of caring will go a long way.

Reward staff for achievements. Give small monetary awards to employees who lose a pre-designated amount of weight, quit smoking, stick to an exercise regime, or achieve another personal goal. Their achievement will translate into productivity for the organization.

TO HELL WITH BURNOUT

Typically nonprofit staffs are overworked and underpaid. Frequently they're "sick" and "tired" too. They love their organizations; they volunteer long hours; they trade high salaries for internal satisfaction. They can only keep it up so long. Eventually exhaustion and burnout set in.

Unfortunately, organizations watch burnout occur and do nothing about it. Many actually encourage it by expecting staff to work long hours for the cause. "I was saving the world but losing my family," said one executive director. His board and staff knew it was happening but didn't stop it. They expected him to work that hard. They worked that hard too. After years of not dealing with the exhaustion, both the director and staff lost their morale and their vision. The organization has had to cut back its operation.

Employee burnout, unchecked, is as dangerous as incompetence. Watch for it and reduce it by building revitalizers and rewards into your personnel system.

Staff sabbaticals. Send people away for a week or a month to study with an expert in your field, to take a course, to get new ideas. People need to be refreshed. The only requirement should be a minimum of three years service.

Mental health days. Require staff to take "well" days several times a year. Staff who don't choose their own can be "banned" from work by their supervisor.

Organization-paid coursework. Nourish your staff by encouraging them to take courses. Pay all or part of their tuition. Mary Kay Cosmetics pays for employee courses based on the grade they earn: 100% for an A or B; 75% for a C; 50% for a D; nothing if the employee fails.

The Goal Line Stand Award. Even more than raises, staff members need recognition. They work hard for your organization and they want to know you know. An award that draws on the football analogy of tough times in the trenches, enables you to recognize that staff member who had a tough week but survived. It acknowledges that individuals screw up, suffer defeats, but remain valued and competent.

Each of these suggestions provides a way for you to let your employees know you appreciate them — as human beings, not just as employees. For more suggestions, read the latest best sellers by business gurus; read Inc. and Fortune magazines; talk to personnel directors in local corporations. Better yet: think about what you'd like an employer to do for you.

Here are some more simple, inexpensive recognition devices borrowed from the corporate sector and the book *100 Best Companies to Work for in Canada.*[8]

Omark Canada, Ltd. bolsters its employees' savings plans by matching every employee dollar with 50 cents.

Vancouver City Savings Credit Union gives employees a rose on their birthdays and on their anniversary of joining the organization.

Speedy Muffler King sends roses to the spouse of each employee on his or her anniversary. They also offer scholarships for employees' children.

Shoppers Drug Mart managers catch their employees "doing something right." They announce names and good deeds at quarterly staff meetings. All commended employees are entered in a drawing for a free trip for two to Florida.

TEAMWORK AND DECISION-MAKING

Nonprofits tend to plan poorly and decide slowly. Both behaviors are inimical to enterprise. As we've said before, enterprise requires strong organizational planning and streamlined decision-making. Cultivate those behaviors by systematizing them.

Plan regularly and frequently. Adopt an annual planning process that begins halfway through the fiscal year. Start the process with several institution-wide meetings at which you develop your large plans for the coming year. Then have each department develop its plan, in detail, to support the organization plan. Finally, merge the department plans into a coordinated, comprehensive, achievable institutional plan. Four months into the plan, update it at both the department and institution levels.

Offer decision-making to as many levels as possible. The people who implement programs are the best able to plan and budget for them. By doing so, they will "buy in" to the goals and work even harder to achieve them.

Budget after you plan. Use the final institutional plan to develop budgets for each department. Budgeting should be the last step in the planning process, and should be completed and approved before the start of the fiscal year.

Produce and use monthly financial statements. They are the only way you'll know if you are deviating from your projections. Follow deviations immediately with mid-course corrections. The end of the year is too late to bring the budget back in line.

Implement a 30/60/90 day decision-making structure. Anything truly worth doing can be decided quickly. Create a timeline for ventures (and all major decisions) based on three 30-day checkoff points. At the end of each 30-day period ask yourself if the data suggests you should go forward or not.

Allow yourself time to properly gather, study and digest information. But no more than 90 days. By the end of that time you should have enough information to know whether a venture is worth pursuing. You should have done common sense testing of the idea; gathered information on the industry; developed rough costs and income possibilities; and tested the idea on potential corporate partners. If, armed with that information, you are not compelled to jump headfirst into the project, don't do it — the benefits probably don't outweigh the risks. Stalling the decision won't change that. Some ideas are meant to be left undone. Better the idea than you.

Checklist:
Characteristics of an Entrepreneurial Nonprofit

1. Staff are given responsibility and the power to carry it out.

2. Goals are clear; the ways to meet the goals are left to individuals.

3. All staff share the organization's vision, goals, philosophy and style. They trust each other to implement programs.

4. Criticism is sought — and freely rejected.

5. Staff is ego-healthy, self-confident and able to make decisions quickly. People that lack these attributes don't last long.

6. Staff enjoy being somewhat overwhelmed; they thrive on internally-created pressure.

7. There is laughter, rowdiness and other physical outlets for tension — belying the hard work and high expectations below the surface.

8. Staff meetings are regular, required, and democratic. Everyone shares what they're doing, and usually, food as well. The staff takes turns leading the meetings.

9. The organization has a strong culture. People fit or they don't. If they don't, they leave quickly.

10. The organization is predictable in the way people are treated; unpredictable in the new and unusual challenges that lead to quality programs.

11. The organization is not afraid of conflict and tension, but requires staff to offer solutions along with complaints.

12. The organization encourages staff to grow, and to leave when their learning curve has leveled off.

13. Staff are willing to risk and try new things. They are not afraid to fail.

14. Staff are passionate about their work and the organization.

---

15. Staff constantly challenge assumptions, asking "why do we do this? Is there a better way?"

16. Staff seek criticism from others whose opinions they trust. They also feel free to "strategically ignore" some of what they hear.

17. Problems are seen as opportunities.

18. The staff believes in the enterprise philosophy.

19. There is no tolerance for whiners or wimps.

20. Key staff thinks conceptually *and* in specifics.

21. The organization is seen as an experimental laboratory, constantly evolving and fostering new learning opportunities.

22. The organization hires specific skills on contract instead of putting people on payroll.

23. The organization knows their customers well.

24. The organization has a bias toward being different — and better — than other organizations.

25. The organization works with clients repeatedly, getting them involved in the organization so they come back for more.

26. The organization is pro-active: they go to people with an idea rather than waiting for someone to come to them.

27. Organization staffers and management are impatient.

28. They plan ahead and project how each department's plans will affect the others'.

29. They believe that people work best on their own interests.

30. Managers do "grunt" work at times because it builds an egalitarian culture.

31. All staff — including top managers — work the "front desk" regularly to stay in touch with customers.

32. Praise is sincere and free-flowing.

33. There is no apparent physical hierarchy in the offices.

34. Staff's jobs grow with them. There is no expectation of climbing a job ladder.

35. Managers hire staff who are smarter than they are, looking at an applicant's qualities not his qualifications.

CHAPTER 34:

Enterprise And The Board

"A company is judged
by the president it keeps."
—James Root Hulbert,
American educator

"Along this tree
From root to crown
Ideas flow up
And vetoes down."
—Anonymous

TOP TO BOTTOM PHILOSOPHY

First and foremost: don't do enterprise if your board doesn't agree. They will kill it — and most likely you — in the process. If they don't buy the concept, educate them. Give them this book. Remind them how much money you need them to raise this year. Wait until a majority of your board members — including the most influential ones — approve the concept before undertaking it.

Even after your board approves, you will need to continue educating them. They will have the same concerns your staff has. They will fear that you will start sacrificing quality for money. They'll fear you'll lose your mission. Answer their concerns just as you do those of the staff.

Remind your board of the benefits of enterprise; that enterprise empowers your organization to get its message heard. It generates unrestricted revenue. It enables you to do programs you can't currently afford. Remind them that quality is nonnegotiable and that programs staff will be voices of conscience for all earned income ventures. Use the pictures of your new ventures to infuse the board with the excitement and potential of your vision.

Just as you encourage the expression of staff concerns, encourage your board to question the direction. Don't let their misgivings fester, because they can poison the process and the organization.

Use your board Enterprise Champion to help with the education process. Ask him to speak at meetings. Ask him to invite board members to breakfast to discuss the new direction. As other members join the team, recruit them to woo the reluctant ones.

Like staff, your board will be concerned by change. They may be wary of enterprise not because it's bad, but merely because it's different. As they start seeing results, as they get wowed by your new vision and the broadening of possibilities it brings, most will become as excited about enterprise as your staff.

A few may never adjust. Let them go. Some of your oldest board members may have the hardest time. They've had a hand in creating the organization as it currently is; accepting something different may be too hard. As their terms expire, ask them to leave. That isn't easy, but as with staff, both the organization and the individual will be better off.

RECRUITING NEW BOARD MEMBERS

As board members leave you have the opportunity to replace them, and that is an empowering opportunity for an entrepreneurial nonprofit. Bring on savvy business people. They will apply their skills to furthering your goals, and you will prove to the world that you do what you say. This is one more opportunity to make your vision and your promise real.

You have told the world you are the best organization in your area of specialty. Now use your board members to prove it. Don't just recruit people locally. Go to the best individuals in your field. If you're as good as you say you are, they'll want to join you. Their names on your board will prove to the world that you are what you promise in your slogan.

We are not suggesting that you recruit a figurehead board. No nonprofit can afford to do that. You need all your board members to work for you, to apply their skills to your activities, and still, of course, to raise money. We are suggesting you think big. Make a grid of the skills, credibility and expertise you need to make your vision real. Then go to the best person in each area to fill your needs.

CREATING ADVISORS

Help educate your board and begin the transition to enterprise with a Marketing Advisory Group. This is a team of five to seven people – one key staff person, one key board member, and the balance highly respected talent from areas in which you need expertise, such as:

marketing of consumer goods

printing

sales

advertising, etc.

Ask them to meet two or three times a year at most, only when you have pressing problems for them to address. Their role is to stretch your problems into opportunities by applying their expertise and guiding your business thinking. Make each meeting an hour and a half and give it a targeted agenda which is sent to them in advance.

Encourage their repeat participation by keeping the meetings short and sticking to the agenda.

The Marketing Advisory Group will lend credibility as well as expertise. Your board will be impressed by the involvement of respected business professionals. Their involvement may sway reluctant board members to the enterprise camp and may encourage them to use their own business skills in more entrepreneurial ways. Corporations you approach for partnerships will be impressed at the caliber of business associates you have. Group members may also provide contacts for joint ventures.

The Marketing Advisory Group is also a good way to bring capable business people onto your board. After a year of advising you on enterprise, they will be well cultivated for filling board vacancies.

CHAPTER 35:

Enterprise And Fundraising

*"Business is a combination
of war and sport."*
– Andre Maurois,
The Life of Disraeli

NEW! IMPROVED! FUNDRAISING!

Enterprise does not mean you never have to fundraise again. That skirmish goes on. But it does mean you won't fundraise in quite the same way. Donations may always be an important part of your income pie – but because diversification is the goal, donations should never form as large a part as they do now. You will still talk to corporations and foundations about contributions – but you will talk business first and contributions last. You will talk to them about special projects – ever-conscious that projects will be components of your multi-year vision, not isolated activities. You will talk about general operating support – while inviting them to invest in a diversified, entrepreneurial organization, not asking them to support a worthy cause.

Once you're in the enterprise mode, fundraising becomes one more entrepreneurial activity. It reflects the same proactive vision and carries the same market-minded message as everything else you do: you no longer wait for handouts; you no longer expect things because you are "good;" you go to corporations and foundations with an offer of what you can do for them. Your days of sophisticated begging are over.

SHIFTING BETWEEN FUNDRAISING & ENTERPRISE

Fundraising can mesh with enterprise, carefully and comfortably. The coordination rests in the relationship between your Development Director and your Director of Enterprise. These two will need to work closely together. (In very small organizations where the Executive Director initially plays both roles, it will be very close indeed!) Planning is critical if the two people are to avoid stepping on each others' toes, and instead, strengthen each others' positions.

The coordination between these two departments begins with your organization's annual plan. Look ahead at the projects you plan to do this year, earned income and not, and decide which corporations and foundations you will approach for each. The lists don't need to be mutually exclusive. You can approach one corporation with both venture and fundraising options (as long as you don't present more than three). In fact, that may improve your chance of getting funds. There will be times when your development director will go alone with only funding options. There will be times when your enterprise director will go alone with only venture possibilities. There will be times when the two will go together with a combined menu of options. The important thing is for them to coordinate their activities. Don't ever be in a position where your development director talks to a corporation about a grant while the enterprise director is grooming the corporation for a venture. Clear communication and mutually agreed upon strategy makes fundraising and enterprise smooth, effective partners. They drive an efficient organization.

Generally when you approach a corporation – even if you're hoping for a straight donation – it makes sense to start with marketing options. You still want to impress the corporation with your business sensibilities. You want to single yourself out from the crowd. If the corporation is uncomfortable with enterprise they can always choose to give you a grant. Nevertheless, you want to give them the choice.

Just as you want to lure donors into becoming members, buyers and visitors, you want to encourage corporations to broaden their association with you. They may start as funders, but your job is to make them event sponsors, product partners, and service partners. Your goal is to develop a long-term relationship with them in which they invest in your organization multiple times and multiple ways.

ALWAYS AN EYE ON YOUR VISION

Your fundraising efforts should support your vision. You will spend a lot of time and energy educating the public about who you are, what you do and where you're going. When you ask them for money, make sure they know how it will speed you to those goals. Use your slogan and visuals in your fundraising brochures. Remind people about the projects you've done and those you plan to do. That makes your vision real to everyone involved. Tie each fundraising effort directly to at least one aspect of your vision so people have a concrete opportunity to help you reach it.

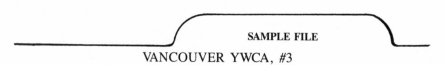

SAMPLE FILE

VANCOUVER YWCA, #3

At the Vancouver YWCA, all major fundraising efforts are directed toward their initiative, Service 2000, providing services to women in need. To make this clear to the public, the YWCA are creating a Service 2000 Fund. All money in the Fund is used to provide services to women in need. They then created a variety of fundraising vehicles which give different audiences opportunities to contribute to the fund.

One of the vehicles is the annual "Pioneer's Reunion." The Reunion taps the nostalgia and altruism of the YWCA's oldest supporters. The YWCA's earliest mission was serving women in need. Many of the men and women who helped it in those days are still around. The Reunion offers them a chance to get together, reminisce about the old days, and by contributing to the Service 2000 Fund, insure that their early pioneering goals are still being met.

Another vehicle, the $100 Club, invites a broader audience to contribute to the Fund. The Club taps people's self-interest as well as their interest in bettering the community. The $100 Club asks members to invest $100 a year for ten years. The money is deposited in the Fund, where the principle accrues interest and the interest is used to provide services to women in need. Club members may withdraw their money after five years, however their accrued interest remains with the Fund. Few people will actually withdraw it, and even those who do know they've helped the Fund grow.

A third vehicle invites people to "insure" the provision of services to women in need by giving them a chance to purchase a life insurance policy naming the YWCA as beneficiary. A portion of each premium is then donated to the Service 2000 Fund.

Through all these vehicles, the YWCA reminds people about its vision. It offers concrete proof that it is achieving its goals. And it invites multiple audiences to help them do it.

CHAPTER 36:

Enterprise And Taxes

"Nothing in life is to be feared.
It is only to be understood."
— Marie Curie,
chemist and physicist

MYTH IS A FEMALE MOTH

Myths and fears abound about nonprofits, earned income and taxes. They're urban legends — like alligators in New York City sewers — that are passed around the country without much basis or documentation. Hopefully, this chapter will lay many of your misconceptions to rest, for while the tax code is complicated, it need not be intimidating. It has a lot of gray area (confusing even to tax attorneys and the IRS). But if you choose to see it as such it can be just as enabling as limiting. So cheer up! What follows is a brief explanation of the aspects of the code that affect nonprofit enterprise.

THE CURRENT TAX CODE

The current IRS code allows nonprofits several avenues for generating nontaxable income. Museums run gift shops and travel programs; hospitals run restaurants and pharmacies; colleges rent dorm rooms and computers; social service agencies sell counseling to corporate employees . . . and few of them pay tax. As long as a business venture is substantially related to an organization's mission its income will be exempt. It is possible, legal (and absolutely ethical) to earn large amounts of income and not owe any tax. Here's why.

The tax code that governs nonprofit earned income specifies three characteristics a nonprofit activity must meet *in order to be taxable.*

- It must be "unrelated to the organization's tax-exempt mission."
- It must be "regularly carried on," and
- It must be deemed a "trade or business."

If an activity meets all three of these criteria, its income will be subject to UBIT — Unrelated Business Income Tax. Few ventures meet all three.

TRADE OR BUSINESS

The "substantially related" test is by far the most important. To be substantially related to an organization's mission, a venture must contribute in an "important way" to the furthering of that mission. It must not exist solely to make money. According to that definition, the operation of an off campus fast food franchise by a university is not related, but the sale of textbooks is, because textbooks further the university's purpose of educating students.

Income from a catering business run by a history museum is not related, but income from Victorian dinners such as those held at the Molly Brown House in Denver *is* related, because such dinners further the Museum's purpose of educating people about history.

To be "regularly carried on," an activity must be ongoing, not occasional. If it is comparable to commercial activity – such as the running of a store – then it is likely to be considered "regularly carried on". By this definition, the operation of a store is regularly carried on, chances are a one-time special event will not. Obviously many nonprofits generate tax-free income from stores which are regularly carried on. They are able to do so because the stores sell merchandise that is related to their missions, or because they meet one or more of the exceptions explained below.

The purpose of these regulations is not to keep nonprofits from operating a trade or business. Nonprofits can run related businesses that are not taxable. Their purpose is to keep them from running an ongoing business that exists solely to make money, and which would compete unfairly with taxable businesses.

Unfortunately (perhaps fortunately!) none of these criteria is absolutely clear. Like many things in law, the code leaves a great deal open to interpretation. This lack of clarity leave nonprofits a fairly wide berth for operating untaxed earned income activities.

BUSINESS, BUT NOT TAXABLE

A Nonprofit can run an unrelated business that is not taxable if the business meets one of the following criteria:
- Is the activity conducted primarily by volunteers? If so, it is probably exempt.
- If the activity involves the sale of merchandise, has substantially all of the merchandise been donated? If so, it is probably exempt.
- Is the activity carried on primarily for the convenience of your members, students, patients, officers or employees? If so, it is probably exempt.
- Is the activity producing "passive income", such as rents, royalties or dividends? If so, it is probably exempt.

These exceptions are what permit many nonprofits to realize substantial untaxed profits from ongoing businesses. Hospitals, for example, earn untaxed income from the portion of their pharmacies that are operated for the convenience of patients.

Service organizations generate untaxed revenue in thrift shops because the thrift shops are run by volunteers and sell merchandise that has been donated.

Museums make untaxed money from restaurants because the restaurants exist for the convenience of museum visitors.

DETOURS AND SHORTCUTS: PROPOSED CHANGES

Because so many nonprofits have made money from untaxed businesses, a coalition of small business owners has challenged the IRS code, claiming it is too lenient. They charge that nonprofits compete unfairly with small businesses because they don't pay tax on their revenues.

They further claim that only 7% of the nonprofits that do owe taxes actually pay. In response to these charges, the House Ways and Means Oversight Committee held hearings to examine possible changes in the tax code. While no one knows exactly what the Congress will propose, most people agree that the code will undergo changes, probably some time in 1989.

Much of the focus of the investigation is the "substantially related" test. Under the current code, the IRS can identify individual activities within an operation as related or unrelated. Each activity's income is then taxed, or not taxed, accordingly. Under the proposed regulations, these activities would be more closely scrutinized. The committee is considering tightening the definition of relatedness.

The Committee is considering applying UBIT to the sale of individual products and services not directly related to an organization's mission, and to publics other than those explicitly stated in an organization's charter. Some of the activities that might become taxable under a revised code are:

- within hospital pharmacies: income from lab tests, prescriptions and equipment sold to other than in-patients;
- within university bookstores: income from sales to people other than students;
- within nonprofit health and fitness centers: income from facilities not available and affordable to the general public.

The relatedness of income from affinity credit cards, advertising and property rental is also under scrutiny by the Committee.

Another focus of the investigation is subsidiaries. The Committee is considering recommending that the IRS look at a nonprofit's "family" of organizations in order to determine if it is entitled to tax-exempt status. If the "family" is weighted toward profit-making activities, the tax-exempt status of the organization might be questioned. This might negate the benefit of establishing a for-profit subsidiary to shelter an earned income activity.

The House Committee is also considering changing the definition of a "controlled subsidiary" by more strictly regulating the types of transactions they tend to do. Currently a nonprofit can maintain 80% control of an incorporated subsidiary. Under the proposed changes, that control could decline to less than 50%. This would create a disincentive for nonprofits to create separate subsidiaries since they would have less control over their operations and income.

NEW TAX FORMS?

A third focus of the investigation is on the tax form itself. Parallel with the Committee's investigation, the IRS is considering revising the tax form itself. The proposed form would require more detailed information about the sources of the income and about the nature of the activities that generated it.

RELAX

While these possible changes sound ominous, they need not be for several reasons:

1. The proposed changes are just that – proposed, nothing more. The issue is still before Congress; proposal modifications are occurring all the time. We won't know the extent of the changes for a while.

2. The proposed changes are not designed to keep nonprofits from earning income. They are merely designed to keep them from competing unfairly with tax-paying businesses. The Committee is trying to isolate the areas in which nonprofits are directly competing with business, and level the playing field by taxing those activities.

3. The proposed changes (as well as the current law) affect only those activities that are unrelated to an organization's mission. That's not what this book is about. If, as our book suggests, you use related earned income ventures to further your goals, taxes will not be an issue. Your ventures, like the ventures described here, will be inherently, purposely, substantially, related to your mission.

4. The proposed changes do not threaten an organization's tax-exempt status unless its unrelated income far outweighs its related income. Again, the ventures described in this book are related and shouldn't place an organization at risk.

5. Nowhere in the tax code – current or proposed – does it say a nonprofit can't earn income. The code merely states that unrelated income will be taxed. Yet nonprofits fear taxes as they would a plague. Taxes are just another expense. If you are considering an unrelated venture, calculate the amount of tax you will have to pay on its earnings and include that on the expense side of your pro forma. If the venture still earns a reasonable profit, do it!

You can view the tax code as punitive or enabling. If you see it as punitive, you will lament the things you cannot do. Look instead at the things you can! The range of related activities is tremendous. If you're concerned about the relatedness of a venture you're considering, consult an attorney who is familiar with the code. Make him your ally in determining what you can do and what you can't. If need be, pay tax. The field of nonprofit enterprise is full of possibilities for organizations that are proactive, innovative and willing to take a calculated risk. Grab the opportunities!

CHAPTER 37:

What Light Through Yonder Nonprofit Breaks?

"There was a young lady named Bright,
Whose speed was far faster than light;
She set out one day
In a relative way,
And returned home the previous night."
—*Punch*, December 19, 1923

Our society is rapidly changing. From a marketing point of view, we are already well into the 1990s. Business is geared up to sell its dream. It has already identified Yuppies as a mere fraction of the Babyboomers who will continue to constitute the new decade's major consuming group.

Do you know where your constituents are tonight? Entrepreneurial nonprofits do. They will be no less amazed at some of the emerging trends than the rest of society, but they won't be surprised by them. Many enterprising nonprofits will harness and set trends themselves. As consumer groups become more splintered, corporations will need to be more proficient at finding them. Your organization can be a great resource for this and an influential social force, too.

Early in this book we discussed creating change rather than watching it. We hope we have offered some tools – and sparked some fantasies – that will assist you in your mission. Baseball writer Roger Kahn was recently approached by a disgruntled fan at a minor league game. "They aren't very good," said the fan of the minor league players. "Good enough to dream," replied Kahn.

Are you?

ENTERPRISE WORKSHEET

This worksheet will help you consolidate the ideas you've gotten from this book into a list of ventures your organization might pursue. If you get stuck while filling it out, or if you come up with an idea you're not sure will work, give us a call, or mail your completed worksheet to us. We'll be happy to help you—**for free!**

> AddVenture Network
> 1350 Lawrence Street, Plaza H
> Denver. Colorado 80204
> (303) 572-3333
> Fax (303) 572-3355

1. DEFINE YOUR MISSION: NARROWLY and BROADLY.

You're used to defining your mission narrowly. Defining it broadly may help you recognize new areas for action, new audiences to serve and new partners to work with.

> example: National Crime Prevention Council
>
> *narrow mission:* to help people protect themselves from crime at home and in the street
>
> *broad mission:* to help build stronger communities. This includes: fighting child abuse; drug education; involving businesses in protecting their neighborhoods and employees; and building bridges between community groups.

Define your mission:

    narrowly: _____

    broadly: _____

2. TAKE STOCK OF YOUR ASSETS

List your organization's assets, including: credibility, expertise, individual staff skills, physical assets, programs, print and media pieces, etc.

_____

_____

3. WISH LIST

What programs, products or services do you wish your organization could do?

_____

_____

4. TAKE STOCK OF YOUR AUDIENCES

Current: (who do you serve now?)

_____

Future: (who *else* needs or wants what you do?)

_____

5. WHO WANTS TO DO BUSINESS WITH YOU?

What businesses serve the same audiences you do? List them. They're all potential partners because you can help them look good to their customers.

_____

_____

6. WHAT CAN YOU DO FOR. . .?

Given your broad mission and assets, what can you do for each of the businesses you've listed above? What kinds of programs, products or services can you offer that will help them attract customers *and* spread your message?

_____

_____

WHO NEEDS OR WANTS. . .?

Look at your assets and wish list again. What businesses might want those things to help build their own business?

_____

_____

8. REPACKAGING

What do you already have (or do) that, with a little repackaging might meet a business's need?

_____

_____

9. ENTERPRISE BLUEPRINT

Fill in the chart below to create an "enterprise blueprint" for your organization.

PRODUCTS	YOUR VENTURE IDEA	AUDIENCE GROUP	CORPORATE BUYERS
Publications			
Tapes, video			
Kits			
Calendars			
Posters			
Maps			
Others			
SPECIAL EVENTS			
SERVICES Instructional			
Others			

10. PRIORITIZE YOUR VENTURES

Of all the ventures on your chart, which are the easiest to pursue?
- Check the top few against the "9 Criteria" (page 106).
- Choose one or two to start with.
- Establish a 30/60/90 day decision schedule for those.

ENTERPRISE CALENDAR

task	month 1	month 2	month 3
1. select Enterprise Champion	X		
2. complete "Year 3 Questions"	X		
3. develop vision statement	X		
4. hire copywriter to craft vision slogan	X		
5. hire artist to illustrate vision and ventures	X		
6. develop strategy for communicating vision to multiple publics.		X	
7. educate staff and board about new direction		X	
8. hire Director of Enterprise, create Enterprise Department		X	
9. prioritize possible ventures according to 9 Criteria		X	
10. establish 30/60/90 day decision schedule		X	
11. proposal circulating for 1st venture			X
12. spirit of enterprise infusing organization			X

INDEX

NOTES

[1]*What They Don't Teach You At Harvard Business School*, Mark H. McCormick; Bantam Books, 1984.

[2]*The Baseball Hall Of Shame*, Bruce Nash & Allan Zullo; Pocket Books, 1986.

[3]*The Misfortune 500*, Bruce Nash & Allan Zullo; Pocket Books, 1988.

[4]Gunnar Madsen, Richard Greene & Mark Pritchard; Best of Breed Music Publishing, 1986.

[5]*The Nonprofit Venture Reporter*, Initiative on Nonprofit Entrepreneurship; New York University, Fall 1988.

[6]Wm.Robinson & B.Rogers; Jobete Music, BMI.

[7]*In One Day*, Tom Parker; Houghton Mifflin, 1984.

[8]*The Financial Post selects the 100 Best Companies to Work for in Canada*, Eva Innes, Robert L. Perry, Jim Lyon; Totem Books, Toronto, 1986.

ABOUT THE AUTHORS

Richard Steckel played Executive Director at the Denver Children's Museum for almost eight years. Under his leadership, the Museum moved from near bankruptcy to earning 95% of its operating budget. Since starting AddVenture Network in 1984, he has been an "enterprise coach" to over 60 nonprofit and for profit corporations in the United States, Canada and Great Britain.

Robin Simons is a consultant in exhibit design for museums, and in marketing and management for nonprofits. She is the author of four other books on a startlingly wide array of subjects.

Peter Lengsfelder is the consommé writer. His concoctions have satisfied marketing taste-makers and magazine readers alike. Today, his stock and tirade is producing nourishing television in San Francisco, where the fog is often soupy.

Design by Design and Image Communications, Denver, Colorado.

Allow us to introduce ourselves...

Between Ten Speed Press, Celestial Arts, and Audio Literature we offer over 400 books, posters, and tapes covering everything from business to cookery, rainforests to surfspeak. Some of our more popular titles include:

BOOKS

What Color Is Your Parachute
by Richard N. Bolles

The bestselling yearly guide to finding a job or changing careers. $12.95 paper, 488 pages

The Moosewood Cookbook
by Mollie Katzen

A beloved vegetarian classic. $13.95 paper, 248 pages

The Surfin'ary
by Trevor Cralle

A definitive dictionary for surfers, with wild color photos and drawings. $19.95 paper, 256 pages

Love Is Letting Go of Fear
by Gerald Jampolsky

This simple and effective bestseller is a guide to leading a happier life. $7.95 paper, 160 pages

Self Esteem
by Virginia Satir

A series of affirmations that help develop a sense of self worth and confidence. Also available as a poster. $5.95 paper, 64 pages; 23 x 35, poster $3.95

TAPES:

The Education of Little Tree

Read by Peter Coyote, this tape illuminates Native American values and spirituality. $15.95, two cassettes

The Screwtape Letters

Monty Python member John Cleese is a hilarious "senior devil" in C. S. Lewis's satire of religious pomposity. $15.95, two cassettes

POSTERS

All I Really Need to Know I Learned in Kindergarten

Colorful presentation of Robert Fulghum's bestselling essay. 23 x 35, $3.95

Rainforest Posters

A series of four gorgeous high-quality prints show the wildlife of four rainforest zones: South America, Africa, Asia, and the Pacific Northwest. 23 x 35, $11.95 each or $40 for the set.

Ten Speed Press / Celestial Arts Available from your local bookstore, or call
Box 7123   Berkeley, CA 94707   or write for our free complete catalog.
(510) 845-8414